30 LESSONS TO LEAD

FROM BREAKDOWNS TO BREAKTHROUGHS

DAVE REGGINA

30 Lessons to Lead / Dave Reggina — 1st ed.

ISBN: 979-8-9991744-0-6 (pbk)

ISBN: 979-8-9991744-1-3 (eBook)

Book Cover Design: Debbie O'Byrne | Jet Launch

Book Format & Design: Mary Bellettieri | Mary Belle Books

Author Photography: Claudio Valenzuela | Cayivisions

www.davereggina.com

To my daughter, Kali Michelle Reggina —

If there's one thing I hope you remember about your dad, it's this:

I was a leader.

Not just in title, but in how I showed up.

How I treated people. How I kept going, even when it was hard.

How I lived with purpose, not just for myself—but for you.

You changed my life, baby girl.

You changed the way I love.

You changed the way I lead.

You made me want to be better in every room I walk into—

so that one day, when you walk into your own, you'll know exactly what it looks like to lead with strength, compassion, courage, and heart.

This book is filled with lessons I've learned through struggle, growth, and grace.

But the most important one?

You.

You are my reason. You are my reminder. You are my legacy.

I love you more than words can ever say.

—Dad

30 LESSONS TO LEAD

CONTENTS

PART THREE
LEAD TO MULTIPLY

THE REASON I LEAD

Before you dive into the first lesson...

Before you pick up any strategy...

Before you try to master leadership, discipline, or communication...

I want to be clear about where *my* foundation comes from.

For me, nothing moves forward without God.

Not my healing.

Not my growth.

Not my purpose.

Not this book.

But it wasn't always like this.

I didn't start with unwavering faith and I didn't grow up grounded in spiritual confidence or deep alignment with God. It took over thirty years of searching, stumbling, breaking, and rebuilding to get here. Years of pride, years of pain, and years of trying to muscle my way through everything on my own but God never stopped pursuing me—even when I was running in the opposite direction.

On April 27, 2025, I was baptized and publicly gave my life to Christ.

That moment didn't make me perfect, but it made me whole.

It didn't erase the past, but it redeemed it.

It didn't make life easier, but it gave my life eternal meaning.

I don't force my faith on anyone, and I never will, but I also won't shy away from the truth that God has been the greatest reason I've been able to endure, rise, and lead.

I'm a disciple of Jesus Christ. While I know everyone comes from different backgrounds, belief systems, and upbringings, I want to be upfront—my life is evidence of divine grace.

Too many things have aligned.

Too many doors have opened when they shouldn't have.

Too many moments were saved, not by my strength, but by something far greater.

There were years where I was broken—physically, emotionally, and mentally.

Years I was lost in my own pain, my own habits, and my own ego.

Somehow, despite all that, I'm here today writing this book.

Leading others, coaching transformation, raising my daughter with intentionality, and speaking on stages that once felt out of reach.

That's not coincidence. That's God.

FAITH ISN'T JUST BELIEF—IT'S ALIGNMENT

You don't have to subscribe to my faith to gain value from this book. These thirty lessons are designed for all people but I'd be doing a disservice if I pretended I got here by willpower alone.

Every time I thought it was over, I prayed.

Every time I had no answers, I surrendered.

Every time I got too far from who I was meant to be, I was pulled back by something I couldn't explain.

I've come to learn that leadership without alignment is empty.

You can have the money, the followers, and the success but if you're not grounded, you'll lose it all.

My grounding is God.

My alignment is faith.

My power flows from that place—not ego, not credentials, not perfection.

A HUMBLE INVITATION

This isn't a religious manual, it's a leadership book. However, I couldn't open it without acknowledging the One who made it possible.

Whether you believe in God, the universe, energy, or something entirely different, I encourage you to connect with whatever helps you stay grounded in something bigger than yourself.

Because when you lead with humility...

When you remember you're not in control of everything...

When you seek purpose over popularity...

That's when real transformation begins.

WHY GOD ISN'T A LESSON—HE'S THE LESSON

I decided against making this the first lesson in this book, because for me, God doesn't belong in a chapter.

He is the cover, the foundation, the spine, and the through line of this entire journey.

I've seen Him show up when I had nothing left.

I've felt peace when the storm should've drowned me.

I've been redirected, protected, and restored in ways that logic could never explain.

So no, this isn't a lesson.

This is the reason *behind* every lesson.

I wanted you to know that before we start.

If you're walking through pain, doubt, fear, or confusion right now, hear me clearly...

You're not alone.

There's a plan for you, even if you can't see it yet.

There's purpose in the pain, and strength on the other side.

There's power in starting exactly where you are.

I've watched God turn my breakdowns into breakthroughs and if He can do it for me, He can do it for you, too.

Let's lead with faith and let's build with purpose.

Let's begin this journey *together*.

PART ONE
LEAD YOURSELF FIRST

SELF-DISCIPLINE
THE FOUNDATION OF LASTING SUCCESS

Self-discipline is the ability to control your thoughts, behaviors, and emotions in the face of temptation and distraction. It's not the flashiest trait, it doesn't win awards or trend on social media, but it's the veiled line that ties together every meaningful success story.

In fact, self-discipline is the great separator. It's what turns potential into performance, intentions into results, and chaos into clarity.

Without it, even the most talented individuals drift, delay, or self-destruct. *With* it, you can achieve nearly anything you set your mind to.

WHY SELF-DISCIPLINE MATTERS

In today's world, distraction is the default. We're flooded with dopamine hits—social media, streaming shows, endless notifications, constant noise. Everything around us is designed to pull us away from what actually matters.

That's why self-discipline is more critical than ever. It's the internal compass that keeps you locked in on your mission, even when life tries to steer you off course.

Whether you're trying to transform your body, grow your business, write a book, or become a more present parent—there will be moments when you simply don't feel like showing up. That's the difference-maker.

Discipline doesn't care how you feel, it responds to what you value. It reminds you of your standards, even when your emotions scream otherwise.

Here's the truth—no one is coming to save you. There's no perfect time and no secret shortcut. There's only the decision to take action, even when it's hard. *Especially* when it's hard. That's what builds character and leadership.

THE EVERYDAY POWER OF DISCIPLINE

Discipline isn't just found in life's defining moments—it's built in the daily grind and lives in the little choices you make when no one's watching.

It's getting out of bed when the alarm goes off and saying no to the easy way out. It's showing up to train, to create, and to lead, when your body says rest and your mind says quit.

Those decisions may seem small, but they stack over time. They create momentum and they shape your mindset. They become your reputation with others, but more importantly, with yourself.

Discipline gives you something no external source ever can—*self-respect*.

When life punches you in the mouth, when you're tired, stressed, or hit with setbacks, it's discipline that keeps you upright. It becomes your anchor. You don't spiral, you recalibrate, and you keep swinging.

With discipline, progress becomes inevitable because consistency always outpaces intensity.

I want to pause here and give credit to someone who lives this truth at the highest level—Ed Mylett. If you've ever heard him speak, you've probably heard the phrase: "One more." One more rep. One more call. One more disciplined act when your body and mind beg you to quit. That mindset isn't hype—it's leadership. It's a commitment to not let your feelings dictate your future. Ed's approach reminds us that greatness isn't built on what you feel like doing, but on the actions you choose when it's most inconvenient. I carry that with me every single day.

DISCIPLINE SETS THE STANDARD IN LEADERSHIP

Leadership isn't about charisma or cleverness—it's about consistency.

If you lead a team, a family, or even just your own life, your discipline sets the temperature for everything else.

People won't follow your words—they'll follow your habits, they'll mirror your effort, and they'll feed off your example.

When your people see you showing up early, staying focused, prioritizing growth, and following through on promises—they'll trust you. Not because of what you say, but because of what you do.

The most powerful leadership doesn't need a title. It's earned through disciplined actions repeated over time.

The opposite is also true. If you compromise your own standards, others will follow that pattern. Discipline doesn't just build you—it builds your culture.

A SKILL YOU BUILD—NOT A TRAIT YOU'RE BORN WITH

Here's the truth most people miss—self-discipline isn't something you either have or don't, nor is it encoded in your DNA.

It's a skill, which means it can be developed by *anyone*.

It begins with small wins like making your bed, drinking water before coffee, and sticking to your plan even when you're tired. These tiny wins become building blocks of a new identity.

Before long, you start thinking differently, acting differently, and even walking differently, because you're not just someone who *wants* discipline—now, you're someone who *embodies* it.

Start by getting clear on what matters to you and then, reverse engineer daily systems that support it. Remove distractions, automate the basics, establish boundaries, and build friction between you and bad decisions.

Most importantly, don't wait to feel ready. Readiness is a byproduct of action. You don't *wait* your way into greatness, you *discipline* your way into it.

PERSONAL STORY: THE ALARM THAT CHANGED EVERYTHING

I'll never forget the morning that changed my life.

It was 4:30 AM. My alarm went off like it always did but this time was different.

I didn't hit snooze and I didn't negotiate. I just sat up, swung my legs over the bed, and said, "Let's go."

It was one tiny choice, but it became the foundation for everything that followed.

That morning routine—4:30 AM wake-ups, morning workouts, journaling, intentional time—became my daily contract. One small win led to another. I started walking with more purpose, thinking with more clarity, and living with more intention.

Out of that rhythm, the *No Snooze Podcast* was born. Today it's ranked in the top 10% of podcasts worldwide. Back then though? It was just me and two of my best friends recording in a basement, talking about not hitting snooze on life, on goals, or on responsibilities.

The name wasn't marketing. It was a declaration, a lifestyle, and a refusal to delay purpose.

That discipline? It didn't just transform my mornings. It transformed me.

What I've learned is this—greatness doesn't come from big speeches or perfect conditions. It comes from small, quiet decisions made consistently over time.

That alarm clock didn't just wake me up—it woke up the leader in me. The same can happen for you, if you're willing to rise when it rings.

FINAL THOUGHT

Self-discipline isn't restrictive, it's liberating. It frees you from regret, from shame, and from the constant battle between what you want now and what you want most.

In leadership, discipline is your superpower. It's what earns respect when pressure rises. It's what allows you to lead yourself and others with integrity.

You don't have to be the smartest, strongest, or most experienced. You just have to be willing to show up, day after day, when others won't.

Success isn't random, it's earned through self-discipline.

ACTION STEP: OWN YOUR MORNING

Starting tomorrow, commit to one disciplined act first thing in the morning—**don't hit snooze.**

When your alarm goes off, get up immediately with no delay and no second guess. Then take one small positive action—make your bed, drink water, stretch, or review your goals.

That first win creates momentum and reinforces your identity. It sets the tone for the day and your leadership.

Track your streak. Go for seven straight days. Don't aim for perfect, aim for proof that you're becoming the kind of person who gets up and gets after it.

REFLECTION QUESTION

When the alarm goes off tomorrow...

Will you choose comfort—or will you choose to lead?

SETTING GOALS
THE ROADMAP TO ACHIEVEMENT

Without a goal, you may be moving, but not necessarily anywhere meaningful. Setting clear, specific goals is one of the most powerful tools you have for creating structure, direction, and momentum in your life.

Goals are not just dreams, they're commitments. They give you a roadmap to follow when the path gets noisy, unclear, or difficult. They transform hope into a plan, confusion into clarity, and potential into progress.

WHY SETTING GOALS MATTERS

In a world that constantly pulls your attention in different directions —between endless notifications, meetings, and daily distractions— goals help you anchor your energy and focus.

Without goals, you're reacting to life, drifting aimlessly, caught in the currents of circumstance. *With* them, you become the driver of your own journey, choosing your direction with intention and control.

Goals give you clarity and help you cut through the noise, and eliminate distractions. They demand prioritization, forcing you to channel your time, energy, and resources toward what actually moves the needle.

More than that, goals shift your mindset from "someday" to "this is how I'm getting there." They turn vague desires into a concrete blueprint.

Research confirms this power. A landmark study by Dr. Gail Matthews at Dominican University found that people who write down their goals and share progress with an accountability partner, are 42% more likely to achieve them. Writing down your goals activates your brain's reticular activating system—the part responsible for focus and motivation—making you naturally alert to opportunities that support your mission.

Goals are more than wishful thinking, they're neuroscience-backed tools that reprogram your brain for success.

BRINGING GOALS TO LIFE

It's not enough to want something. Goals must be specific and actionable. Consider the difference between saying, "I want to get in shape," versus, "I want to lose ten pounds in thirty days by working out thirty minutes per day and eating high-protein meals."

One is a hope; the other is a strategy.

Powerful goals break down into daily, manageable actions. This is where most people fall short—they dream big, but never shrink it down to size. Without clear steps, overwhelm sets in and progress stalls.

When you know exactly what to do each day, progress becomes inevitable, the journey becomes predictable, and momentum builds.

For leaders, this translates into setting clear targets for their teams and themselves, creating measurable Key Performance Indicators (KPIs), and using accountability systems. The discipline of breaking goals into bite-sized chunks mirrors how great leaders break down big challenges into manageable wins.

MENTAL TOUGHNESS THROUGH GOALS

Every meaningful goal comes with resistance such as obstacles, discomfort, and moments when quitting seems easier.

These trials are where mental toughness is forged. Every time you push through, you reinforce your belief in yourself. You prove that you can honor your word, follow through, and keep momentum alive, even when it's hard.

Goal achievement isn't just a checkmark on a to-do list, it strengthens your identity and creates a version of you that you can trust to show up.

It's this trust in self, this confidence built in the crucible of challenge, that's the bedrock of leadership. Leaders don't just direct others—they direct themselves first.

THE FORMULA: SPECIFIC + MEASURABLE = ACTIONABLE

Vague goals don't create results. Saying, "I want to be more productive" is too abstract to move the needle.

Saying, "I will finish this project by Friday at 3:00 p.m.," turns intent into action. It creates clarity and urgency.

The more specific and measurable your goals are, the more effective they become. Add structure, give them deadlines, and break them down into chunks so small they're impossible to ignore.

Instead of "I want to write a book," say "I will write five hundred words every morning, five days per week, until the manuscript is complete."

This approach converts vague intentions into disciplined habits that deliver results.

PERSONAL STORY: FROM $10K TO REAL ESTATE—HOW A SIMPLE BREAKDOWN CHANGED MY LIFE

In 2014, I made a decision that changed everything—I was going to save $10,000.

At the time, I was working three jobs. My social life was nonexistent. Late nights out were traded for early mornings meal-prepping and I tracked every dollar obsessively.

I broke down the goal to a science:

$10,000 per year = $833 per month

$833 per month = $208 per week

$208 per week = $29 per day

Once I saw it that way, it stopped feeling impossible. It became a game I could win—one disciplined day at a time.

This goal wasn't just about money. It was about proving to myself that no matter how big a target seemed, it could be conquered with the right mindset and strategy.

That $10,000 was the seed that grew into a $100,000 investment account. That capital became the down payment on my first real estate property.

More than the financial gain, the lesson was life-changing. It taught me to break any big challenge into daily steps and to honor those steps no matter what.

I remember one winter night, exhausted after work and tempted to skip my weekly budget review, feeling the pressure of burnout. Nevertheless, I reminded myself of my goal breakdown. I pulled out my spreadsheet, recalculated my progress, and recommitted. That moment of choosing the goal over comfort forged a resilience that rippled through every area of my life.

Since then, this lesson has permeated every leadership role I've held. I've seen teams crumble without clear goals and thrive when direction is precise. One vivid memory stands out. Early in my career, leading a team project without a clear goal, we wasted months in confusion and finger-pointing. Once we reset with a sharp, measurable target and a clear breakdown, morale skyrocketed and results followed. The contrast was a lesson in leadership clarity I never forgot.

That's the power of clear goals—they give you a path through the noise, even when the road gets tough.

FINAL THOUGHT

Goals are more than a to-do list, they're your leadership roadmap.

They transform dreams into plans, intentions into action, and potential into progress.

When you commit to setting specific, measurable goals and break them into daily steps, you take control of your future. You build mental toughness, self-trust, and momentum that no obstacle can stop.

Leadership is not born from chance—it's built step by step, goal by goal.

ACTION STEP: WRITE IT, BREAK IT, START IT

Take five minutes today to set one specific, measurable goal you want to achieve.

Write it down.

Break it into monthly, weekly, and daily steps.

Get clear on your numbers and get clear on your routine.

Then take the first action—*today*.

You've just made your vision tangible. Now, let's make it real.

REFLECTION QUESTION

What's one goal in your life that seems too big to start until you break it down?

TIME MANAGEMENT
MASTER YOUR MOST VALUABLE RESOURCE

Time is the one thing you can never get back. No matter how successful, rich, or influential you become, you can't add more hours to your day. This makes time management not just important but absolutely essential for high performance. It's the difference between spinning your wheels and making significant, purposeful progress.

WHY TIME MANAGEMENT MATTERS

We all have the same twenty-four hours in a day, yet some people seem to accomplish far more than others. The difference? Time management. It's not about working harder or longer hours, but about how you prioritize, structure, and use your time. Without good time management, you'll find yourself constantly overwhelmed, running from one task to the next without ever feeling like you've truly accomplished anything meaningful.

Time management gives you control. It's about being intentional with your time, making sure that the most important tasks—those that align with your goals—are given priority. When you manage your time well, you create space for the things that matter most, whether it's advancing your career, building stronger relationships, or simply improving your own health.

HOW TIME MANAGEMENT TRANSLATES TO LIFE

In everyday life, time management means making intentional decisions about where to invest your energy. How much time are you spending on activities that don't move the needle forward? Whether it's scrolling through social media, watching TV, or attending meetings that don't serve your bigger goals—time is lost in those moments, and it's time that you'll never get back.

When you start to manage your time with purpose, you see results. Think about your daily routine. When you plan and structure your time, you have more clarity and energy. It's easier to focus, accomplish tasks, and feel a sense of satisfaction at the end of the day. On the flip side, when your time is scattered, it's easy to feel drained, disconnected, and unproductive.

Time management allows you to be proactive rather than reactive. Instead of waiting until the last minute or scrambling to catch up, you're in control of your schedule. You get to decide what deserves your attention and what doesn't. You intentionally carve out time for your most important goals, and as a result, you make consistent progress, day by day.

THE LEADERSHIP MINDSET BEHIND TIME MANAGEMENT

Mastering time isn't just about tools or hacks—it's a mindset shift. Leaders who master their time see it as a sacred resource, not a disposable commodity. This mindset forces you to evaluate every commitment through a critical lens: *Does this move me closer to my purpose or pull me away?*

When you adopt this mindset, you start saying "no" more often to distractions, low-value meetings, even well-meaning requests. Saying no isn't about being difficult—it's about protecting your ability to say yes to the things that truly matter. This discipline in boundary-setting is often what separates great leaders from good ones.

BOUNDARIES ARE NOT BARRIERS — THEY'RE BRIDGES TO LEADERSHIP SUCCESS

Many people confuse boundaries with selfishness, but boundaries actually build trust and respect. When you protect your time, you're signaling that your work, your health, and your relationships deserve your full presence. This clarity makes your team and loved ones respect your leadership more.

Clear boundaries reduce burnout by preventing overload. Burnout is often the result of poor time management combined with unclear limits which leads to exhaustion, poor decision-making, and damaged relationships. Leaders who master their time—and their boundaries—are more resilient and capable of leading others through stress and uncertainty.

REST AND RECOVERY: THE OFTEN-OVERLOOKED ASPECT OF TIME MANAGEMENT

A hidden gem in time management is making room for rest. Too many leaders fall into the trap of equating busyness with effectiveness, forgetting that recovery fuels productivity and creativity. Quality rest—sleep, breaks, mental downtime—is non-negotiable.

Studies show that even short breaks during work restore cognitive function and reduce fatigue. Leaders who prioritize rest return to tasks sharper, more innovative, and better able to handle pressure. Time management is as much about knowing when to pause as when to push.

TIME MANAGEMENT AND EMOTIONAL INTELLIGENCE: A QUICK PREVIEW

Managing your time well also impacts your emotional intelligence— the ability to understand and manage your own emotions and those of others. When you control your schedule, you reduce stress and over- whelm, which helps you stay calm and present. This presence allows you to read others accurately, respond thoughtfully, and build deeper connections which are core qualities of effective leadership.

To keep this lesson focused, I'll dive deep into emotional intelligence in a dedicated future lesson. For now, know this—mastering your time expands your capacity to lead with empathy and clarity because you have the mental space to be fully present.

THE POWER OF PLANNING YOUR DAY

Effective time management starts with planning. The most successful people don't leave their day to chance—they plan it. They know what needs to be done and *when* it needs to be done.

This is where the magic happens. Instead of reacting to whatever life throws at you, you're proactively making choices about how you spend your time. Every night, take five minutes to plan the next day. This can be as simple as a list of your top three to five priorities for the day. When you have a clear roadmap of what needs to be done, you won't waste time trying to figure out what to focus on, you'll simply hit the ground running.

Additionally, batching similar tasks together (like answering emails or creating a to-do list) is another strategy to save time. It helps you avoid the constant switching between tasks, which can drain your mental energy.

OVERCOMING TIME WASTING

One of the biggest obstacles to time management is time-wasting. We all have habits or distractions that eat up precious minutes or hours, whether it's excessive screen time, procrastination, or inefficient habits. The first step to effective time management is identifying and eliminating these distractions.

You can begin by tracking how you spend your time for a few days. You might be surprised at how much time is spent on activities that don't serve your goals. Once you know where your time is going, you can begin to make conscious decisions to minimize these distractions and reallocate your time to things that matter.

PERSONAL STORY

I thought I understood time management—until I became a father.

In a co-parenting setup, I had my daughter three to four days per week. During those days, everything fell on me—bathing, feeding, comforting, playing, teaching. Most men never experience the full load of daily parenting alone, especially with a toddler, but I did.

Back when I was in a two-parent household, I never realized how much flexibility I had. Time felt like it was always available. I could work late, get up early, and do things on my own terms. But when that changed, I quickly learned that time is not something you manage passively, it has to be structured with intention.

I learned that the hard way. I had a massive work presentation lined up—a program and budget pitch to a major organization. It was a career moment I had prepared for but in the chaos of managing my daughter's schedule, my schedule, and everything in between, I double-booked and missed the entire meeting. I didn't realize it until it was too late.

I was sick over it. Not because I missed the meeting, but because it exposed a brutal truth—time management can't be a part-time habit. If you don't run your schedule, your schedule will run over you. That experience taught me to build structure around my life, no matter what. If I wanted to lead at a high level, I had to manage my time like my life depended on it.

FINAL THOUGHT

Time doesn't pause for anyone—not even leaders. In the end, it's not how much you did that matters most, but whether what you did was aligned with your mission. You don't need more hours in the day. You need more intention in the hours you already have. Mastering your time is how you build trust with yourself. It's how you create space for what matters most—your purpose, your people, your peace. When you manage your time with purpose, you don't just get more done—you become someone worth following—because how you spend your time, is how you spend your life.

ACTION STEP

Spend five minutes today identifying your biggest time wasters. Then, plan one concrete action you can take to eliminate or reduce these distractions tomorrow. Reclaim your time, and you'll start reclaiming your life.

REFLECTION QUESTION

Where in your life are you confusing busyness with progress and what would it look like to take back control of that time?

GROWTH MINDSET
THE FOUNDATION OF LIFELONG PROGRESS

Your mindset is the lens through which you see every opportunity, obstacle, and outcome. Few shifts are more powerful and more transformative than the move from a fixed mindset to a growth mindset.

This isn't about positive thinking or blind optimism, it's about choosing a belief system that makes progress inevitable.

A growth mindset is the unshakable belief that you are not limited by your current abilities, intelligence, or circumstances. It's the understanding that who you are today doesn't have to define who you'll be tomorrow and that effort, learning, and persistence are the true ingredients of greatness.

In leadership, this is the foundation. Quite simply, if you don't believe you can grow, *you won't*, and if you don't believe others can grow, you'll never lead them well.

WHAT IS A GROWTH MINDSET?

Stanford psychologist Carol Dweck, who pioneered this concept, defines a growth mindset as the belief that abilities can be developed through dedication and hard work. This view creates a love for learning and resilience that are essential for great leadership.

Conversely, a fixed mindset assumes that talent and intelligence are static—you either have it or you don't. This belief system breeds fear of failure, fear of feedback, and fear of discomfort.

Here's the real difference in practice:

- A fixed mindset says, "I'm just not good with people."
- A growth mindset says, "Communication is a skill I can improve with effort."
- A fixed mindset says, "I'm terrible with money."
- A growth mindset says, "I haven't learned how to manage money yet—but I can."

That one word—*yet*—can become a lifeline for any leader willing to lean into discomfort and keep going.

WHY IT MATTERS IN LEADERSHIP AND LIFE

Your mindset is either a ceiling or a launching pad. If you see failure as the end, you'll stop short every time things get hard. If you see failure as feedback, *as information*, you'll keep showing up, even when results are slow or setbacks hit.

And remember, they *will* hit.

Leadership isn't about avoiding failure, it's about how you respond to it. Only a growth mindset gives you the fuel to persist.

President Abraham Lincoln is a case study in this. Before he became one of the most revered leaders in American history, he lost eight elections, failed in business twice, and suffered a nervous breakdown, but he didn't stop. He reframed failure as education. He didn't see losses, he saw lessons, which was a mindset that helped him develop into the leader who would hold the country together during its darkest hour. That's the power of belief married to resilience.

In your leadership journey, whether you're guiding a team, raising a child, or rebuilding your life—your mindset will determine how far you're willing to go.

HOW IT SHOWS UP IN REAL LIFE

In fitness, a fixed mindset says, "I'm not athletic," and walks out of the gym after a tough session. A growth mindset says, "I'm getting stronger every day," and keeps showing up.

In business, a fixed mindset avoids feedback out of pride. A growth mindset craves it because it knows feedback sharpens the blade.

In parenting, a fixed mindset worries about getting it "right." A growth mindset focuses on staying consistent and learning along the way.

In relationships, a fixed mindset gets defensive when criticized. A growth mindset leans into tough conversations to grow deeper connection.

HOW TO BUILD A GROWTH MINDSET DAILY

You don't just "have" a growth mindset. You build it like a muscle and you reinforce it through repetition, awareness, and choice.

Start with your language:

- Replace "I'm bad at this" with "I'm working on this."
- Replace "This is too hard" with "This is challenging me."
- Replace "I failed" with "I'm still figuring it out."

When you hear yourself slipping back into a fixed perspective, pause, take a breath, and ask—*Is this really a limit or just a challenge I haven't figured out yet?*

Over time, those micro-adjustments create macro-growth. They change your identity, they build resilience, and they unlock potential that was waiting just beneath the surface.

PERSONAL STORY

I didn't always believe I could grow. For years, I thought my past was a permanent setback. I had made decisions that weren't just bad—they were reckless.

There was a season in my life where my nights were filled with clubs, bottles, and bravado. I spent money that I didn't have trying to be a man I wasn't. I was chasing validation, not a vision.

When I began trying to shift—when I started reading, learning, stepping into leadership—I felt like an imposter. Who was I to lead anyone? Who was I to talk about growth when I had wasted so much time?

Through years of therapy, coaching, and reflection, I realized something profound—my worst chapters weren't proof that I was broken, they were proof that I was becoming.

The shame that once haunted me? I now wear it as a badge of perspective.

The mistakes I made? They're my fuel for compassion, clarity, and conviction.

When someone tells me they've messed up their shot, I don't flinch. I look them in the eye and say, "You're not done yet."

That's the power of a growth mindset. It doesn't erase the past, it repurposes it.

FINAL THOUGHT

Every leader wants more influence, impact, and achievement but none of those things happen without growth. More importantly, growth doesn't happen without belief.

A growth mindset is the ultimate multiplier. It changes how you train, how you lead, how you love, how you think, and how you bounce back when it all falls apart.

If you want to lead at a high level, it starts *here* rather than with talent or strategy.

It starts with *belief.*

ACTION STEP

Identify one area of your life where you've been telling yourself, "I'm just not good at that." Now, reframe it. Write down a growth-focused version of that belief. Speak it out loud, repeat it daily, and then prove it through action.

REFLECTION QUESTION

What belief have you internalized that's holding you back and what would it look like to rewrite it through the lens of growth?

LESSON 5
ACCOUNTABILITY
THE DISCIPLINE MULTIPLIER

Accountability isn't just about being held to a standard or checking a box. Accountability is about consciously choosing to live by standards so high and personal that they demand regular checks, honest feedback, and total ownership—especially when no one else is watching. Accountability is the invisible, relentless engine that transforms good intentions into daily habits, discipline into momentum, and leadership into a lasting legacy. It's the difference between making promises and actually keeping them, and between dreaming and doing.

In any high-performance environment, whether that's leading a business, transforming your body, or navigating life's toughest challenges —accountability isn't punishment or shame, it's a privilege. It's the tool that builds resilience when motivation fades and fatigue sets in. When discipline runs dry, accountability fills the gap and keeps you moving forward, step after gritty step, toward the goals that matter most.

WHY ACCOUNTABILITY IS ESSENTIAL

You can have a crystal-clear vision, you can be naturally talented, and you can even have ironclad discipline, but without accountability, all those assets plateau and decay over time. Why? Because human nature is wired to drift. It rationalizes when things get hard, it looks for excuses when energy dips, and it lets you off the hook when frustration or fear hit. That's why the difference between the person who starts and the person who finishes is accountability—the system that pulls you back when your brain tries to quit.

Accountability puts a guardrail around your standards. It adds a level of commitment that goes beyond the fragile willpower of any individual moment. It forces clarity on what you're really doing, demands follow-through, and opens you up to feedback—sometimes tough, but always necessary. It's the invisible push that athletes get from coaches, that entrepreneurs get from mentors, that anyone serious about growth gets from a trusted accountability partner. A simple text or call asking, "Did you do what you said you would today?" can be the single factor that changes your entire week, month, or year.

TYPES OF ACCOUNTABILITY THAT MATTER

Accountability isn't one-size-fits-all. It comes in three powerful forms, and when you combine them, you create a triple-threat that crushes excuses and accelerates progress:

1. **Self-Accountability:**
   - This is the hardest kind. It's the quiet voice inside that says, "No one's watching, but I'm doing this anyway." Self-accountability is built by making promises to yourself—and then keeping every single one, even when it sucks. Self-accountability is trust in your own word. Without it, nothing sticks.

2. **Peer Accountability:**
   ○ This is your crew—people who see you at your best and your worst and still demand more. They're the ones who call you out when you start slacking, celebrate your wins, and hold the line so you don't fall into mediocrity. Peer accountability is raw, real, and necessary. It's the difference between going it alone and thriving together.
3. **Coach or Mentor Accountability:**
   ○ This is the external, structured form. A coach, mentor, or formal program creates a system where your progress is tracked, challenged, and refined. There's no place to hide or half-ass it. Discipline is specifically engineered for growth.

THE HIDDEN POWER OF BEING CALLED OUT

Accountability lives in truth—and truth isn't always comfortable. Being called out can sting and it can shake your ego, but if you're serious about growth, that sting is one of the highest forms of respect you can receive. It means someone believes in your potential enough not to let you settle for less than you're capable of.

Instead of shying away, lean into those moments. Invite accountability by telling someone your goals, asking them to check in, and giving them permission to call you out when you start to slip. This isn't a sign of weakness—it's strategic humility. It's the fast track to resilience, clarity, and lasting growth. Isolation is a trap and accountability is *freedom*.

ACCOUNTABILITY IS A MIRROR

Most people avoid accountability because they're afraid to face the mirror it holds up, but that mirror—cold, honest, and unfiltered—is the exact tool you need for transformation. Accountability reflects your actions back to you, with brutal objectivity and relentless consistency.

It's how you measure real progress beyond the hype or excuses and how you build unshakable consistency. It's how you lead with integrity, not just when it's convenient but when it's damn hard. True leadership isn't about the spotlight or the applause—it's about showing up day after day, even when you're tired, frustrated, or nobody's watching.

PERSONAL STORY

Co-hosting the *No Snooze Podcast* wasn't just a creative project—it became one of the toughest and most transformative accountability experiences of my life.

We weren't celebrities and we didn't have a massive production team or any guarantees that people would even listen. We were just three regular guys—Mike Parelli, Claudio Valenzuela, and myself—trying to do something real, something consistent, and something that could create impact.

But let me tell you the truth—there were *countless* mornings I wanted to quit.

There were weeks where life felt heavier than the mic in front of me. Times when my Crohn's flared up, times when the weight of fatherhood, leadership, and everything in between left me drained. There were moments I'd finish work, come home exhausted, and the last thing I wanted to do was prep another outline, hit "record," or re-watch our footage for notes.

But we had a system—a system that *saved us*.

Mike and Claudio held each other accountable with scheduling. They'd lock in the dates, the time, the location—no excuses. What was my role? I was the structure guy. The night before every episode,

I made sure we had a clear topic and a rough outline. That one-pager became our blueprint.

It wasn't about inspiration, it was about responsibility.

We didn't always feel like recording, but we did it anyway. It wasn't just for us. We did it because *we said we would*. We did it because *we knew people were counting on us*. That's what accountability does—it pushes you beyond your excuses and into your commitment.

Here's the wild part—that same system still exists.

Even now, after Mike stepped away from the show, Claudio and I *still* use that same accountability framework. We still prep the night before, we still schedule weeks in advance, and we still hold space for each other to show up—no matter what life is throwing at us.

Accountability has become more than a system for us. It's a way of life. It's the quiet contract we signed—not with a network, but with each other and most importantly, with ourselves.

What most people miss is this—*you can't lead others, if you can't hold yourself accountable first*. Yes, we built a podcast, but what we were really building was discipline, trust, consistency, and follow-through.

To this day, every time I hit record, I'm reminded that motivation may get you started but accountability is what keeps you going.

FINAL THOUGHT

Accountability isn't about being policed or punished. It's about taking ownership and committing to the grind of growth every damn day. It turns "I'll try" into "I will." It creates momentum, demands ownership, and pushes you to rise above excuses and tap into your full potential.

No high performer gets there alone. The most successful leaders are the ones who own their actions, seek accountability, and never settle.

ACTION STEP

Choose one person to hold you accountable this week—whether it's your workouts, your leadership habits, or your daily routine. Share your goal, ask them to check in regularly, and commit to reporting back honestly. Remember, growth explodes when accountability is in place.

REFLECTION QUESTION

Where in your life are you avoiding accountability and what's really holding you back from inviting it in?

What's one small step you can take today to embrace accountability instead of running from it?

LESSON 6
EFFECTIVE COMMUNICATION

SAY LESS, MEAN MORE

Communication is *everything* but it's not just about opening your mouth and making noise. Communication is about transferring clarity, intention, and meaning so that the person on the other end *actually gets it*. Whether you're leading a team, coaching a client, navigating a difficult relationship, or simply trying to be understood by your child, how you communicate is the single most important factor that separates influence from noise, trust from doubt, connection from confusion.

Here's the brutal truth—most people don't really communicate, they *broadcast*. They speak to be heard, not to be understood. They're thinking about what to say next while the other person is talking. They throw out words hoping something sticks. This kind of one-way noise creates barriers, misunderstandings, and resentment. But real communication? Real communication is a *two-way street*. Real communication requires intention, focus, and the willingness to listen deeply. If you want to lead yourself and others at a high level, you have to learn this skill. Otherwise, everything else you do is just noise.

THE THREE PILLARS OF EFFECTIVE COMMUNICATION

1. **Clarity Over Complexity**
    - Too often, we try to sound smart by using complicated language or convoluted explanations. Intelligence isn't in the words you use though—it's in how clearly you can make your point. Clarity means stripping away jargon, fluff, and filler so that your message hits like a laser beam. When you say exactly what you mean *simply* and *directly*, you eliminate confusion. Imagine giving your team a vision or giving a loved one a boundary. If it's muddy, everyone drifts. If it's clear, they *move*. Clear communication creates direction and trust, while complexity creates chaos.

2. **Presence Over Performance**
    - Your words only matter if your body and mind show up with them. People can *feel* when you're distracted, half-listening, or mentally drafting your next reply instead of truly hearing what they're saying. Presence means showing up fully—locking eyes, reading body language, and leaning in with intention. It's about *being there* in the moment without distraction. This kind of presence builds trust at a deep level because it tells the other person, "You matter. I'm here." Without presence, even the clearest words feel empty.

3. **Responsibility Over Reaction**
    - Communication isn't just about what you say, it's about how you say it and how you respond. Most conflicts don't come from what was said, they come from how it was heard and how people react emotionally. Leaders don't just react, they respond with control, intention, and ownership. This means you choose your tone, your timing, and your delivery carefully instead of letting

frustration or fear dictate your words. Taking responsibility means owning the impact of your communication, even when it's uncomfortable. This transforms conflicts into conversations, and misunderstandings into alignment.

WHY IT MATTERS IN EVERY ARENA

Communication isn't just a "soft skill." It's the *foundation* of everything worth having in life and leadership. Without it:

- Leadership turns into chaos because nobody knows the plan or feels aligned.
- Relationships break down because resentment builds where understanding is absent.
- Fitness coaching fails when cues are missed or motivation isn't properly conveyed.
- Life becomes a series of missed connections and frustrations that keep you stuck.

Think about your day-to-day. How many times have you been misunderstood? How often have things gone sideways because you or someone else didn't say what you meant, or didn't listen enough? Every time you communicate with clarity, presence, and responsibility, you're rebuilding trust and influence in yourself and your world. If you want to lead well, mastering this skill is non-negotiable.

HIGH PERFORMERS MASTER SIMPLICITY

The greatest communicators don't throw a bunch of words around hoping one lands. They pick their moments. They *simplify* complex ideas into stories, metaphors, and real talk that connect instantly. They speak less often—but when they do, their words land like a hammer on a nail. This isn't magic; it's discipline and deep self-awareness. It's about knowing *exactly* what you want to say, *who* you're saying it to, and *why* before you open your mouth. That way, every sentence moves the conversation forward. This kind of communication creates momentum, trust, and clarity all at once.

PERSONAL LESSON

I learned the hard way what happens when communication breaks down. Early in my career, I supervised an incredible employee— someone who was dependable, talented, and trusted me enough to open up about something deeply personal. She told me her mother was failing to file important paperwork that would allow her to return to her home country. It was a stressful, and emotional situation for her. Instead of showing up fully present, I checked my phone twice, and sat distracted, not fully engaged. I didn't even realize it at the time, but later she told me my body language, and lack of attention made her feel like I didn't care.

She left my office in tears, and I chased her down the hall to apologize. She said bluntly, "You don't care about me." Those words hit me like a freight train. I was mortified. I didn't intend to hurt her, but my lack of presence spoke volumes. That moment was a gut punch and it changed everything. From that day forward, I committed to being fully present in every conversation, to listening actively, and to making sure people know they matter—not just through words, but through actions. Effective communication is the difference between connection and isolation, leadership and failure. I still have a lot to learn, but I've improved my communication so much because of that lesson.

FINAL THOUGHT

Effective communication isn't a one-and-done skill. It compounds over time like interest in a bank account. Every clear message strengthens your influence. Every thoughtful pause builds respect, and very honest conversation deepens connection. You don't have to be the loudest voice in the room—you just have to be the clearest, and most intentional. Talk less, say more, and lead louder.

ACTION STEP

Before your next important conversation, take a moment to write down exactly what you want to say. Cut the fluff and focus on clarity, presence, and responsibility. When you speak, be *intentional*. Show up fully and deliver your message with purpose. That's how you build effective communication skills.

REFLECTION QUESTION

Think back to a recent conversation where you weren't fully present or clear.

What distracted you?

How did your words or actions affect the outcome?

What will you do differently next time to show people they truly matter?

BUILDING RESILIENCE
THE STRENGTH BEHIND THE STRENGTH

Resilience isn't about pretending that pain or struggle doesn't exist. It's about becoming the kind of person who chooses to move *through* the discomfort, the setbacks, and the storms—rather than avoiding or running from them. Resilience is the grit that surfaces when everything you planned falls apart, when pressure builds to unbearable levels, or when life throws unexpected chaos your way. Here's the key—resilience isn't just bouncing back to where you were before. Resilience is about bouncing forward—stronger, sharper, and with deeper wisdom than ever. Studies show that resilient individuals are 30% more likely to report higher life satisfaction, and better health outcomes, proving that resilience is a foundational survival skill.

Resilience is often the true deciding factor in successful leadership practices, relationships, personal growth, and fitness challenges. Talent and timing will get you only so far, but an unyielding tolerance for adversity will fuel long-term success.

WHAT RESILIENCE ACTUALLY LOOKS LIKE

Forget the Instagram version of resilience, which tends to focus solely on shiny victories with zero cracks. Real resilience is gritty, messy, and deeply human. It means showing up to the gym or the office when your mind is screaming for rest and your body aches from exhaustion. It means admitting to yourself and others that you're struggling, but you're still going to make the call or send the email. It's staring down rejection, failure, or harsh feedback and using it as fuel to sharpen your edge rather than as a reason to quit.

It's about taking full ownership, even when blaming someone else would be easier. It's the courage to pivot and adapt when your carefully laid plans crumble, even if it means feeling vulnerable or uncertain. This kind of resilience isn't glamorous, it's built one uncomfortable, raw moment at a time. It's imperfect, relentless, and absolutely necessary.

RESILIENCE IS A SKILL, NOT A TRAIT

Some people seem naturally tough, but here's the truth—resilience is a skill you develop with consistent practice like, building a muscle through reps at the gym. Every time you choose to face discomfort instead of avoiding it, you're repping out your resilience.

You build resilience by stacking hard moments, and honoring your word to yourself, especially when nobody's watching. Every workout finished even though your body begged you to quit and every difficult conversation you refuse to avoid, even if it makes you sweat. When you get out of bed after a crushing setback and decide to keep moving forward—those moments add up. They forge a strength inside you that can weather anything life throws your way.

WHY RESILIENCE MATTERS NOW MORE THAN EVER

We live in a world addicted to convenience and comfort. Discomfort is demonized and we've been conditioned to avoid pain at all costs. But here's the cold, hard truth—you don't grow when you're *comfortable*—you grow when you're challenged and pushed beyond your limits. Resilience is your superpower in a soft, easy world.

Resilient people aren't surprised or broken by hardship—they're prepared. When life shatters plans or blindsides you with crisis, they don't crumble—they build from the ruins. People with higher resilience have a better chance of bouncing back from trauma and stress with sustained mental health.

As a leader, your ability to stay grounded during chaos doesn't just protect you—it gives your team and your family permission to do the same. You model that adversity is not a stop sign, but a stepping stone.

TACTICS TO BUILD RESILIENCE DAILY

Voluntary Hardship

Intentionally seek challenge. Take cold showers, wake earlier than comfortable, or add extra reps to your workout. When you *choose* discomfort regularly, your tolerance builds so that when life forces hardship on you, you respond with strength instead of fear or avoidance.

Reframe Failure

Don't run from failure—study it. Every setback is a teacher. Ask yourself, "What is this moment asking me to learn? What version of me does it demand I become?"

Failure reframed is resilience in training.

Build Recovery, Not Just Grit

Resilience is not white-knuckling through life twenty-four hours per day, seven days per week. It's knowing when to push and when to rest. Recovery—physical, emotional, and mental—is critical to long-term durability. It's the pause that fuels the comeback.

PERSONAL STORY: THE GREATEST LESSON IN RESILIENCE—MY MOTHER'S JOURNEY

For me, resilience isn't just a concept or buzzword—it's deeply personal. My mother, Nanci Reggina, struggled with addiction to drugs and alcohol for most of my life. Watching her fight that battle was one of the hardest things I've ever experienced. Addiction is a brutal, isolating force that doesn't just affect the person using—it impacts the entire family.

She faced years of pain, setbacks, and moments when giving up would have been easier. I know she wanted change long before she found it. Her path to sobriety was far from a straight line. It was ugly, it was hard, and it tested her every day.

What she showed me though, and what she embodies, is true resilience. She did what had to be done, one day at a time, to rebuild her life. Today, nearly seven years sober, she's the best mother and grandmother we could ever ask for—full of love, strength, and wisdom.

Her journey reminds me, and should remind everyone, that it's *never* too late to be resilient. To rebuild yourself no matter how deep the struggle. Nanci's strength and persistence inspire me daily. If we could all have half the resilience she's shown, the world would be a much stronger place. God bless her for being my greatest teacher in resilience and life.

FINAL THOUGHT

Resilience isn't about being unbreakable, it's about being rebuildable and coming back faster, stronger, and wiser after every knockdown. This is what separates those who quit from those who truly become. Every challenge you face is not a barrier, it's your training ground for what's next.

ACTION STEP

Write down the last time you were truly tested.

What did that moment reveal about your inner strength?

What did it build inside you?

Then, commit to doing one thing today that leans into resistance because resilience grows in the uncomfortable places.

REFLECTION QUESTION

Think about a time you wanted to quit but didn't.

What did that experience teach you about yourself?

How can you carry that lesson into your next challenge and show up with even more grit?

TIME FOR REFLECTION
SLOW DOWN TO SPEED UP

In the pursuit of greatness, high performers often live in forward motion chasing goals, chasing time, and chasing what's next. We glorify the grind and we romanticize the hustle but here's the paradox —speed without strategy doesn't lead to breakthroughs, it leads to burnout.

Without pause, even the most determined can end up lost in motion. That's the irony. When you're always moving, it's hard to know if you're even moving in the right direction.

REFLECTION IS THE ANTIDOTE

Let's be clear, this isn't *soft*. It's not just journaling under a tree or lighting candles and meditating. Reflection is a *strategic pause*. It's how you gather data from your own life. It's where pressure transforms into perspective and where mistakes become metrics. Chaos finally quiets and what *really* matters rises to the surface.

In fact, a study from the University of Texas found that reflective writing improved decision-making, emotional regulation, and overall well-being by 27%. Harvard Business School research showed that employees who reflected just fifteen minutes at the end of their workday improved performance by 23% in just two weeks.

This is *performance science*, not philosophy.

Stillness isn't weakness, it's wisdom. It's not a detour from success, it's the direct route to sustainable, values-aligned, high-performance living.

WHY REFLECTION MATTERS IN THE GAME OF GROWTH

Clarity

When you're constantly in motion, it's easy to mistake activity for effectiveness. Reflection helps cut through the noise. It shows you what's actually working—and what you're just doing out of habit. It allows you to move from being busy to being better. As James Clear said, "You do not rise to the level of your goals. You fall to the level of your systems." Reflection exposes those systems and whether they're building you or burying you.

Alignment

Success without alignment is a fast track to emptiness. Reflection helps you ask: *Are my daily actions aligned with my values? My long-term vision? My identity as a leader, parent, or partner?* Without that check-in, you might climb the ladder of success only to find it was leaning against the wrong wall. Research from Stanford shows that values-aligned individuals experience significantly higher levels of motivation, focus, and long-term fulfillment.

Wisdom

Raw experience doesn't create mastery, *evaluated* experience does. Reflection is how you turn the page with intention. It helps you turn past failures into future wins, and past wins into long-term habits. Athletes watch game film, entrepreneurs audit results, and leaders reflect because wisdom lives in hindsight.

THE POWER OF STRATEGIC PAUSES

Most people react but few respond. The difference? *Space.*

Reflection creates that space between stimulus and response. It lets your leadership brain—the prefrontal cortex—kick in. That's the part responsible for long-term planning, emotional regulation, and decision-making. When you reflect, you don't just remember, you recalibrate.

You build leadership muscle by lifting insights, not just weights.

Just like your physical body grows stronger in rest and recovery, your strategy grows stronger in moments of stillness. Reflection is where you breathe, assess, adjust, and then strike with precision.

3 SIMPLE WAYS TO REFLECT EFFECTIVELY

1. Ask the Right Questions

Don't just think vaguely—dig into specifics:

"What did I do well this week, and why?"

"Where did I fall short, and what behavior caused it?"

"What patterns am I repeating—and are they serving me?"

2. Use a Time Anchor

Schedule your reflection like a workout. Link it to a habit—a morning coffee, a drive home, a Sunday reset. Reflection doesn't need to be long, it needs to be *consistent.*

3. Track Patterns, Not Just Events

Events are isolated. Patterns are powerful. Are you always anxious on Tuesdays? Do you crush it after workouts? Is your phone killing your focus? Reflection helps you collect the data of your life and data-driven people make smarter decisions.

MY STORY: THE MOMENT THIS BOOK WAS BORN

In May of 2025, I attempted something I'd never done before—a five-day water fast.

At first, I thought it would be one of the hardest physical challenges I'd ever put myself through. And in some ways, it was. What I didn't expect though, was how internal the real challenge would be. Without the constant routine of eating, snacking, and digesting, there was nowhere left to hide from my thoughts. The noise faded and clarity came right after.

I wasn't fasting for weight loss or performance. I was fasting for guidance and for spiritual alignment. I approached those five days with deep intention, using every window of hunger and discomfort as an opportunity to ask bigger questions: "What's next?" "What am I here to build?" "Where am I being called to lead?"

On day one of that fast during one of my early morning meditation sessions, the concept for this book came to me.

It didn't come as a random idea or a motivational checklist, but as a downloaded assignment. The title, the tone, the structure, and the mission all started to unfold in stillness.

If I hadn't slowed down, I never would've had the clarity to hear it. I would've been too busy grinding to notice the guidance and too stuck in motion to realize the next move.

That fast didn't just reset my body, it reset my leadership, and confirmed a powerful truth—breakthroughs don't always come in motion. *Sometimes they arrive in stillness.*

So, if you're reading this book right now, understand this:

You're holding the product of reflection.

This entire book was initiated in silence—in prayer, in discipline, and in strategic pause.

It's what makes this the most personal story I could possibly share because the words you're reading weren't forced, they were revealed.

Let that be your reminder—sometimes the most powerful progress doesn't come from pushing harder, it comes from listening deeper.

FINAL THOUGHT

In a culture obsessed with doing more, reflection feels radical, but the best leaders, athletes, parents, and creators aren't the ones who *never* slow down. They're the ones who know *when* to pause, *how* to think, and *what* to shift.

Don't confuse motion with meaning. *Fast* doesn't always mean *forward.*

The most dangerous direction isn't backward—it's *forward with no self-awareness.*

ACTION STEP

Take ten minutes today to reflect. Not because you're broken but because you're building clarity. Write down:

One thing you're proud of this week

One thing you want to improve next week

One insight you've gained from reflecting

Then, pause, process, and proceed—with intention.

REFLECTION QUESTION

What's one area of your life or leadership where constant motion has been disguising a lack of direction and what would change if you slowed down to actually listen?

TEAMWORK
SUCCESS IS A SHARED EFFORT

You can go fast alone but you go far together.

There comes a point in every leader's journey where personal discipline, vision, and drive are no longer enough. To build anything of scale or lasting impact—whether it's a movement, a business, a legacy—you need a team. This doesn't just mean warm bodies or cheerleaders either. You need people who challenge you, grow with you, and carry weight beside you.

Teamwork isn't about playing nice, it's about multiplying effort, diversifying strengths, and staying aligned under pressure. It's about creating synergy, where one plus one doesn't equal two, it equals ten.

WHAT TEAMWORK REALLY REQUIRES

It's easy to claim you're a team player but real teamwork reveals itself when tension rises, when plans shift, and when egos could get in the way. It's exactly why most "teams" don't work because the foundation isn't real.

Here's what makes or breaks a team:

Trust

Trust is the currency of high-performance teams. It isn't declared—it's earned through consistent action. When you show up prepared, follow through on commitments, and own your role under pressure, you signal reliability. Great teams run on reliability like engines run on oil.

Role Clarity

There's nothing more damaging to a team than confusion. When people don't know their responsibilities or worse, step outside them, friction and failure follow. Great teams operate like great offenses in sports where every player knows their route, their role, and how it fits the play.

Shared Standards

Culture eats talent for breakfast. Without shared values and standards, even the most skilled individuals will unravel. High-performing teams hold each other to a clear, agreed-upon definition of excellence. When someone slips, they don't coddle, they correct, with care and urgency.

WHY THIS MATTERS EVERYWHERE

In business, companies with highly engaged teams show 21% greater profitability (*Gallup*). Teams that collaborate well innovate faster, serve clients better, and outperform those siloed in individual efforts.

In family, alignment brings unity. Teams aren't just in boardrooms—they're at kitchen tables. Raising a child, supporting a spouse, or leading a household demands communication, shared effort, and emotional presence.

In athletics, championships are never won solo. Michael Jordan needed Scottie Pippen and Kobe needed Shaq (and later Pau Gasol). In sports, you can have a superstar, but dynasties are always built through role players who buy in.

PRACTICAL WAYS TO LEAD AS A TEAMMATE

Define the Mission

Great teams are built on clear missions. What are you all building, and why does it matter? Alignment starts with vision.

Know Your Role and Own It

Be great at your part. If you're the communicator, communicate. If you're the executor, execute. Excellence in your lane inspires trust in the whole team.

Have Hard Conversations

Real teams don't avoid conflict, they use it. Clear the air, speak with truth and respect, and address issues before they metastasize.

Celebrate Wins Together

Recognition fuels retention. Celebrate team success, not just individual effort. People support what they help create.

PERSONAL STORY: BUILDING ACE

When Sean Degnan and I founded Action Cultivates Excellence (A.C.E.), we knew it had to be bigger than us. We had a mission to help men reconnect with their fire and to bridge the gap between masculinity and vulnerability. We also knew that to make it real, we needed a team that *believed* in that mission.

Enter Joe Kay—a man who transformed his life from addiction to leadership through the power of self-discipline and cold exposure.

His program *Ice x Iron* became more than just a method, it became a mindset. He brought his transformation, his belief in community, and his raw experience to the table and A.C.E. was never the same.

Then came Nick Manente, whose military-grade discipline and high-performance background in concierge physical therapy made him the Swiss army knife every elite team dreams of. He worked with top-tier clientele, walked the walk in his own life, and showed up with structure, standard, and strength.

These two didn't just join a company, they *built* it with us. They owned it and they expanded it. Because of their contributions, A.C.E. became a movement, not just a message. That's the power of a real team. People who aren't just aligned on results but aligned on *why* it matters.

The truth? We would've burned out trying to do it all alone. But together, we scaled impact, we grew in depth, and we sharpened each other. That's *teamwork*.

FINAL THOUGHT

Your success will always be capped by the strength of your team.

You can white-knuckle your way to short-term wins—but legacy is built in collaboration.

The best leaders know when to lead from the front, and when to pass the ball.

Because leadership isn't about doing everything—it's about doing *what only you* can do and empowering others to do the rest with excellence.

ACTION STEP

Identify the three most influential people on your team—whether in work, life, or fitness. Send them a message of gratitude today. Then, ask yourself: *What can I do to be a better teammate this week?* Pick one tangible behavior—better communication, clearer delegation, or showing up with more consistency—and commit to it.

REFLECTION QUESTION

What kind of teammate are you right now and what kind of teammate does your vision require you to become?

LESSON 10
ADAPTABILITY
STAY READY SO YOU DON'T HAVE TO GET READY

In a world that changes fast, rigidity breaks but adaptability bends and survives.

Adaptability isn't weakness, it's not indecision, and it's not being tossed by the wind. It's the quiet strength of a leader who can adjust in real time without losing their vision. It's being anchored in purpose but flexible in approach.

The best performers, leaders, and teams aren't the most rigid—they're the most responsive. They can read the moment, pivot with poise, and still drive results when the playbook gets torn up.

WHY ADAPTABILITY IS A LEADERSHIP SUPERPOWER

Life Rarely Goes According to Plan

You can spend months preparing for the perfect launch, the dream schedule, the ideal family rhythm—and life will still throw a curveball. It might be a pandemic, a personal loss, a financial detour, or an unexpected opportunity. Your ability to pivot without panic is what separates stagnation from momentum. Leaders who lack adaptability get stuck, while leaders who embrace it stay in motion.

Adaptability Keeps You Relevant

Industries evolve, teams evolve, and people evolve. If your methods don't evolve with them, you'll become the bottleneck to your own progress. Look around—the landscape is littered with brands, businesses, and people who bet on comfort zones. Kodak invented digital photography and still failed because they couldn't adapt fast enough. Blockbuster laughed off streaming. Relevance is earned through evolution.

It Builds Confidence Under Chaos

Adaptable leaders don't crumble when plans unravel. They get clear, they get creative, and they get to work. Why? Because when you trust your ability to adjust, uncertainty becomes a stimulus not a stopper. You begin to believe in your ability to figure things out, even when the situation isn't ideal.

That's a real leadership edge.

WHAT ADAPTABILITY LOOKS LIKE IN REAL LIFE

In business, when a client backs out or the market shifts, you revise your game plan not your goal.

In fitness, when your travel or work life interrupts your gym schedule, you adjust and squeeze in a thirty minute bodyweight circuit in the hotel room. *Movement over excuses.*

In relationships, when someone you love grows in a new direction, you don't resist you realign, you listen, and you adapt together.

In leadership, when your team dynamics change, or new personalities come in, you don't force the old playbook, you develop new ways to win.

Adaptability doesn't mean constantly changing just to change. It means being *intentionally responsive*, making decisions rooted in purpose, not panic.

HOW TO BUILD ADAPTABILITY LIKE A MUSCLE

Detach from "How" and Stay Anchored to "Why"

Most people cling to their method like it's their identity but real power comes from staying loyal to your mission, not the map. You may need to change tactics, tools, or timelines but never your core reason. Let go of "this is how it's always been," and embrace "this is how it works now."

Train for Uncertainty

The gym builds muscles but so does discomfort. Regularly put yourself in new environments, take on challenges outside your expertise, and stretch beyond routine. Whether it's cold exposure, public speaking, or parenting a toddler—every unpredictable experience sharpens your ability to adapt on command.

Reflect & Respond

Most people either freeze or react emotionally when things change. *Don't.* Instead, pause, and ask, *What's actually changed? What remains true? What are my options?* Then move forward grounded, not frantic. This creates leadership agility—not volatility.

PERSONAL STORY – LEADING IN MULTIPLE LANES

Most people adapt once—after life forces them to.

I've had to build adaptability into my daily operating system.

One hour I'm making strategic decisions in government leadership, managing millions in public funds. The next, I'm coaching high-performance clients. Then I'm hosting the *No Snooze Podcast*, sharing raw truths. Later, I'm giving my full presence to fatherhood, walking into school with my daughter Kali like she's the only thing on the planet that matters. In between that? I'm fielding A.C.E. team calls, launching new programs, managing personal health, and creating content.

This isn't compartmentalizing—it's constant calibrating and it takes real adaptability.

I didn't leave one world for the other. I built a system that allows me to operate in all of them at once. That didn't happen by accident, it happened by design. The key was knowing that no plan survives first contact with the real world.

Every day, I flex, not fold.

FINAL THOUGHT

Adaptability isn't about having all the answers.

It's about staying in the game long enough to find them.

When you build the habit of adjusting with purpose, the world no longer feels like it's happening *to* you—it starts responding *through* you. The mission stays the same and the method evolves.

That's leadership.

The truth is—change is *inevitable* but growth is *optional*.

Those who adapt, *lead*.

ACTION STEP

Think of one area in your life right now where things haven't gone according to plan. Instead of resisting the change, identify one specific adjustment you can make today to stay aligned with your vision.

Flex, don't fold.

REFLECTION QUESTION

What unexpected challenge have you faced recently and how did you adjust in a way that made you stronger?

PART TWO
LEAD WITH INTENTION

CONFIDENCE

"Confidence is the willingness to be as ridiculous, luminous, and vulnerable as you really are."

— *Brené Brown*

Confidence isn't a mask you wear to impress others. It's not arrogance or pretending you have all the answers. Real confidence is a raw, quiet power, and a steady inner knowing that you can face whatever comes, because you've done the work to prepare yourself for it.

Confidence is earned, not given. It's built brick by brick with repeated effort, honest reflection, and unwavering self-trust.

WHY CONFIDENCE IS A BYPRODUCT OF ACTION — NOT WISHFUL THINKING

It's easy to think confidence is some magical trait you either have or you don't but science tells a different story.

The field of psychology, especially research on self-efficacy (the belief in your ability to achieve a goal), shows that confidence doesn't come from compliments, luck, or even positive thinking. It's forged through experience. When you successfully do something, even if it's *small*, you create evidence for your mind that you *can* do it. Over time, that evidence piles up and transforms your belief system.

A 2014 study published in the *Journal of Applied Psychology* showed that consistent practice and mastery lead to significantly higher confidence than motivation alone.

Psychologists Albert Bandura and Carol Dweck explain how "competence loops" form. Success breeds confidence, which breeds more effort, which breeds more success.

In leadership development programs, those who take deliberate, consistent action, *even in discomfort*, build stronger confidence than those who wait for the "perfect" moment or reassurance.

Think about it—if you want to lead with confidence, you have to step into leadership, even when your hands are shaking. If you want to trust your voice, you start speaking *before* you feel ready. Confidence lives in the doing, not the thinking.

THE 3 CS OF CONFIDENCE: WHAT REALLY MOVES THE NEEDLE

1. Competence

Competence is the *foundation*. Confidence begins when you know your craft inside and out and that means studying, training, and sharpening your skills relentlessly. Leaders without competence fake it until they break. Confidence built on a shaky foundation is a house of cards.

Consider this—research by Stanford University found that people who prepared thoroughly for presentations felt significantly more confident, regardless of their prior speaking experience. Preparation breeds competence, which breeds confidence.

2. Consistency

Confidence doesn't come from one or two big wins, it grows in the quiet, unseen moments. Showing up day after day, keeping promises to yourself, and doing the work when no one's watching is where confidence is forged.

The National Institutes of Health states that habit formation can take anywhere from eighteen to two hundred and fifty four days, depending on the individual and the behavior. That means confidence-building is a *marathon*, not a sprint. It's about the small, consistent steps that add up over time.

3. Character

Your character is your internal compass. When you keep your word to yourself and others, you develop self-respect and that self-respect is the bedrock of confidence.

People respect leaders who act with integrity, and more importantly, those leaders respect themselves. When you betray your values or break promises to yourself, confidence slips away like sand through your fingers.

WHAT CONFIDENCE LOOKS LIKE – AND WHAT IT DOESN'T

✔ Shows up with humility and readiness to learn

✘ Doesn't need to dominate the room or be the loudest voice to feel valuable

✔ Acts despite fear and uncertainty

✘ Doesn't wait for the "perfect" moment, plan, or mood

✔ Admits mistakes and moves forward anyway

✘ Doesn't crumble under criticism or setbacks

True confidence is quiet, prepared, and grounded. It's a muscle built by hard-earned small wins, brutal honesty, disciplined habits, and staying in the arena long after others have quit.

THE COST OF WAITING TO FEEL "READY"

One of the biggest traps is waiting to "feel ready" before acting. Confidence rarely works that way. It's not a switch you flip when you suddenly feel perfect. Instead, it's a gradual process of showing up, stumbling, learning, and growing.

Consider the career of some of the world's most confident people. Oprah Winfrey was fired from her first TV job and told she was "unfit for television." Michael Jordan was cut from his high school basketball team. Steve Jobs was once fired from the company he co-founded. None of them waited for confidence, they built it by moving forward despite fear and failure.

Waiting for the perfect moment means you miss thousands of micro-opportunities to prove to yourself you *can* do this. It's those small moments of courage that add up.

PERSONAL STORY – MY JOURNEY WITH CONFIDENCE

When I launched the *No Snooze Podcast*, I was surrounded by incredible leaders like Troy Millings and Rashad Bilal, two mentors who grew up in the same town I now serve as Deputy Commissioner. Week after week, I saw them crushing it—celebrity interviews, international travel, and massive events. Watching the rise of *Earn Your Leisure*, a top financial literacy podcast, was inspiring, but also stirred up envy and self-doubt.

I asked myself, "Am I ever going to get to that level?" But every time, they reminded me that confidence isn't about overnight success—it's about consistent action.

"You're on the right path because you keep showing up," they told me. "The action you take today builds your confidence for tomorrow."

That truth anchored me in moments of doubt. The journey wasn't glamorous. There were times I questioned if anyone was listening or if I even had a voice worth hearing but I kept showing up, episode after episode.

Eventually, they invited me to keynote at *Invest Fest* 2025—the largest financial literacy festival in the world with over 25,000 attendees. The reason wasn't talent alone it was my persistence and my refusal to quit when it got hard.

Confidence isn't pretty and it's not always loud or proud. When you develop the muscle to keep moving forward despite fear, doubt, and setbacks, you build a confidence that no one can take away.

THE SCIENCE OF CONFIDENCE: WHY IT MATTERS FOR LEADERSHIP

Confidence isn't just a feel-good trait, it's a critical factor in leadership effectiveness. Leaders with high confidence are more likely to inspire trust, create alignment, and mobilize teams.

Conversely, low confidence can lead to hesitation, missed opportunities, and a lack of decisiveness, which breeds organizational stagnation.

Neuroscience shows that confidence activates the prefrontal cortex which is the area responsible for decision-making and emotional regulation. It helps leaders stay calm under pressure and think clearly.

The great news? Confidence is trainable. Like strength training for your mind, it grows when you consistently challenge yourself and reflect on your wins.

HOW TO BUILD CONFIDENCE LIKE A PRO

Embrace Imperfection and Fail Forward

Perfectionism is the enemy of confidence. One must accept that mistakes and failures are part of the process. Each failure is data, a lesson that fuels your growth. Adopt a mindset of "failing forward" where every setback propels you closer to mastery.

Celebrate Small Wins

Break your goals into micro-steps. Each time you succeed, no matter how small, celebrate it. This builds positive feedback loops in your brain that reinforce confidence.

Use Visualization and Affirmations

Research shows visualization techniques improve performance and confidence. Spend a few minutes daily picturing yourself succeeding. Couple that with affirmations grounded in reality, like "I am capable because I prepare," to rewire your mindset.

Surround Yourself with Support

Confidence thrives in healthy environments. Seek mentors, coaches, and peers who uplift you, give honest feedback, and celebrate your progress.

FINAL THOUGHT

Confidence isn't a gift you're born with, or a feeling you stumble into. It's the result of deliberate, consistent action, rooted in integrity and competence.

Like a muscle, confidence grows stronger the more you train it. Want the beautiful truth? Once built, it becomes a force no one can take from you.

Leadership isn't about being fearless or perfect, it's about showing up with courage, humility, and relentless self-trust.

ACTION STEP

Identify one area of your life where you've been waiting to "feel ready." Today, take one small, imperfect action that builds trust in yourself. Start your confidence journey through action, not *waiting*.

REFLECTION QUESTION

Where in your life are you still waiting for permission when you already know it's time to move?

LESSON 12
EMPATHY
THE STRENGTH TO FEEL WHAT OTHERS FEEL

In leadership, empathy is often misunderstood as softness. Here's the truth though—empathy isn't weakness, it's *awareness*.

Awareness is **power.**

Empathy is the ability to understand and feel what someone else is going through, even when you haven't lived it yourself. It's about being present, not perfect. It's the muscle that allows you to connect, lead, and influence without losing your edge.

WHY EMPATHY IS NON-NEGOTIABLE FOR MODERN LEADERS

Empathy Builds Trust

People don't follow titles, they follow those who "get" them. Leadership is not about hierarchy or command, it's about connection. You don't need to solve everyone's problems, but if people feel seen and heard by you, they'll trust you. Trust is the currency of leadership.

Empathy Builds Loyalty

Whether at home, in your team, or in business, people stay where they feel understood. You can hold high standards and still lead with compassion. That's not contradiction, that's *mastery*. A leader who can hold *both* accountability and care is a leader people rally behind.

Empathy Helps You Lead Through Conflict

When tension rises, empathy gives you the patience to pause, the courage to listen, and the strength to respond instead of react. It keeps you steady when chaos threatens to shake the ship. Empathy isn't avoiding conflict, it's navigating it with wisdom.

HOW TO PRACTICE EMPATHY WITHOUT LOSING AUTHORITY

Seek to Understand, Not Just Respond

Too often we listen with the intent to reply, not to understand. Real empathy means slowing down, tuning in deeply, and prioritizing connection over quick answers. When you listen this way, you build emotional intelligence, a critical leadership skill.

Lead with Questions

Simple, open questions like "How can I support you?" or "What do you need right now?" send a powerful message that you're here to connect, not control. Questions invite others into the leadership space, build rapport, and foster collaboration.

Validate Without Enabling

Empathy doesn't mean lowering your standards or excusing poor performance. It means acknowledging others' feelings honestly— "I see where you're coming from,"—while holding firm to the expectation that they will rise above the challenge. This balance creates accountability with care.

EMPATHY IN ACTION: WHAT IT LOOKS LIKE

In your marriage, be fully present during stressful moments without rushing to fix everything. Sometimes presence is more powerful than solutions.

On your team, check in with someone whose performance slipped before jumping to criticism. Understand the *why* behind the *what*.

With yourself, recognize your own burnout signs and give yourself grace to rest or recalibrate, without shame or guilt.

Empathy is often what transforms resistance into respect and opposition into openness.

PERSONAL STORY – THE MONKEY BARS AND MY DAUGHTER KALI

One of the most unforgettable lessons in empathy came from watching my daughter Kali on the monkey bars. She was about four years old, just beginning to build the confidence to swing across the bars by herself. Every time we went to the park, we made it a mission —she'd try, I'd encourage, and slowly she got better and stronger.

Then one day, everything changed. Kali suddenly seemed to lose her ability to do it. She tried five times and failed every time. On the fifth fall, she hit the ground hard and began to cry. As a father, I was frustrated *for her* because I knew how much she wanted to conquer those bars, but also because she was stuck.

Instead of rushing her or telling her to try harder, I pulled her aside and I asked her to explain her feelings. At first, she didn't want to talk but when I gave her space, calmed her breathing, and handed her some water, slowly she opened up.

She told me she was mad. Mad because she wanted to show the other kids that she could do it and because she felt like she was failing. All I did was listen. I validated her feelings and told her I completely understood her frustration.

I shared with her a memory from my childhood and how I used to shoot free throws in basketball. I practiced every day, but one day during a game, I missed all six attempts. I was *crushed*, but I didn't quit. I kept practicing, kept shooting, and eventually, I got better.

That moment with Kali was pure empathy. Sometimes all we need is someone who truly hears us, understands us, and tells us, "I get it. *You're not alone.*"

After our talk, Kali said a prayer, asking God to help her get through the monkey bars and you know what? She did it. That day, she not only conquered the monkey bars, she learned what it means to be seen, heard, and supported. That moment bonded us forever.

THE LEADERSHIP LESSON FROM KALI'S MONKEY BARS

Empathy isn't just about kindness—it's a strategic leadership skill that creates trust, builds resilience, and fosters connection. Empathy shows your team and your family you see them—not just their output, but their struggle. It reminds them they're not alone.

Sometimes, empathy means being patient through failure, walking beside people through frustration, and believing in their potential even when they don't see it themselves.

THE SCIENCE OF EMPATHY AND LEADERSHIP

Studies show that leaders who demonstrate empathy create stronger, more engaged teams. Employees who feel their managers care about them are 60% more likely to be engaged at work, driving higher productivity and lower turnover.

Neuroscience also backs empathy as a leadership superpower. When leaders listen empathetically, the brain releases oxytocin—the "bonding hormone"—which promotes trust and cooperation. Empathy literally rewires the brain for better connection.

Yet, only 25% of leaders in a recent Harvard Business Review study were rated as "highly empathetic." This gap represents an enormous opportunity. The leaders who master empathy will have a profound competitive edge because at the end of the day, leadership is influence, and influence flows from connection.

FINAL THOUGHT

Empathy isn't feeling for someone—it's feeling with them.

It's not about agreeing with everyone or losing your edge.

It's about understanding deeply enough to lead wisely and effectively.

In a world full of noise and division, empathy is a quiet strength—a power move that builds bridges, breaks down barriers, and unlocks potential.

If you want to lead people to better, you have to meet them where they are.

ACTION STEP

Have a conversation today where you focus 100% on listening, not *fixing*.

Ask one meaningful question and let the silence do the heavy lifting.

You'll be surprised what people reveal when they feel safe enough to speak.

REFLECTION QUESTION

Think about a recent moment when someone showed empathy to you.

How did it impact your trust, motivation, or confidence?

Now, how can you be that source of empathy for someone else this week?

SELF-CARE
DISCIPLINE, NOT INDULGENCE

Let's clear something up right now—self-care isn't *weakness*, it's a *weapon*.

It's not bubble baths and vacations, it's boundaries, discipline, and knowing when to refuel so you don't burn out.

If you think self-care is selfish, ask yourself—what happens when you run yourself into the ground? Your family pays, your team suffers, and your goals stall. You simply can't pour from an empty cup.

Real self-care is the strategy that sustains your performance—mentally, physically, emotionally.

WHY SELF-CARE IS ESSENTIAL FOR HIGH PERFORMERS

You are your most valuable asset.

Not your resume, not your network—*you*. Your energy, clarity, and capacity determine how well you lead and how consistently you show up.

Burnout disguises itself as hustle.

When you're always grinding but never recovering, performance drops and you don't even notice until it's too late.

Leaders don't just protect time—they protect energy.

Your decisions, your tone, your presence—it all suffers when you're running on fumes. You're either leading from overflow or operating from depletion.

Neglecting self-care is a form of self-sabotage.

You wouldn't let your phone battery die without charging it, so why would you treat your own body and mind any differently? High performers don't wait for burnout, they build guardrails before the crash.

THE DATA DOESN'T LIE: SELF-CARE IS STRATEGIC

Burnout is at an all-time high.

According to a 2022 Gallup study, 76% of employees experience burnout on the job at least sometimes and 28% report feeling burned out "very often" or "always." For leaders, the pressure is even higher because they're carrying the emotional weight of their teams.

Poor sleep kills productivity.

Research from the CDC shows that adults who sleep fewer than seven hours per night are more likely to report chronic health conditions like heart disease, depression, and obesity, all of which reduce executive functioning. A RAND Corporation study estimates sleep deprivation costs the U.S. economy over $411 billion annually in lost productivity.

Cognitive fatigue mimics alcohol impairment.

A study in *Occupational and Environmental Medicine* found that going 17–19 hours without sleep produces impairments equivalent to a blood alcohol level of 0.05%. After 24 hours? It's similar to being legally drunk. You can't lead well when your brain is in a fog.

Recovery improves performance.

Elite military units like Navy SEALs and high-performance companies like Google emphasize recovery because they understand the quality of performance is determined by the quality of recovery. Harvard Business Review reports that leaders who unplug regularly are 23% more productive and significantly more emotionally intelligent.

Neglect leads to decision fatigue.

We make an average of thirty five thousand decisions per day, and without mental recovery, your brain's decision-making power depletes like a battery. Self-care rituals recharge that battery so you can continue making high-quality calls under pressure.

WHAT SELF-CARE REALLY LOOKS LIKE

Non-negotiable routines.

Sleep, hydration, training, and nutrition. The basics aren't boring, they're what keep your edge sharp. You don't rise to the level of your goals, you fall to the level of your habits.

Mental clarity.

Take ten minutes per day to clear your mind through journaling, prayer, silence, or breath work. Stillness isn't laziness, it's leadership prep. Mental fog clouds wise decisions.

Boundaries that protect your peace.

Say no, take breaks, and guard your calendar. Self-care means having the guts to protect your priorities without apology.

Time away to reflect.

Sometimes the best move is to pause, step back, and look at your life from the balcony. That clarity can't be found in constant motion.

People who recharge you.

Surround yourself with those who add energy, not drain it. Conversations with the right people can restore more than sleep ever could.

THE POWER OF THE CHAIR: MY PERSONAL SELF-CARE RITUAL

For a long time, I believed self-care was soft.

I used to think it meant spa days, pampering, or hours of doing nothing. That wasn't me. I was a grinder. I was up early, home late, pushing myself in every area of life. Rest felt like quitting and self-care felt like indulgence. I considered it something that other people did when they had extra time. Not me—I didn't have that luxury.

I was wrong.

Thirteen years ago, I started going to Erwin Gilliam for haircuts. At first, it was just about cleaning myself up—keeping the fade fresh, beard shaped right, and looking good for the week ahead. Over time though, that weekly appointment became something more than a trim. It became a ritual, a reset, and a non-negotiable act of alignment.

Erwin isn't just a barber—he's a brother, a mentor, an entrepreneur, a pastor, and a man who leads with presence and purpose. His shop, *Erwin's Barbershop*, isn't just a place to get lined up—it's a space where men come to reconnect with themselves. There's energy in that room, wisdom in the air, and more authenticity than you'll find in most boardrooms.

For me, that chair became sacred space.

Every Friday, without fail, I block the time. It's on my calendar like an important meeting—because it *is* an important meeting. That forty-five minutes in the chair isn't just about the haircut, it's about regrouping and refocusing, it's where I check in with myself. It's a pause in the chaos, a deep breath at the end of a long week. It's where I'm reminded that how you carry yourself matters and when you look good, you feel good.

More importantly, it's a reflection of something deeper—*intention*.

Consistency in your self-care is a mirror of how consistent you are in life. For me, staying sharp with my cut became a symbol of how I treat the rest of my priorities—with care, precision, and commitment. The same way I show up to lead my team, train my body, love my daughter, and pursue my goals—I show up to that appointment because I've realized something most people overlook.

True alignment means caring for all parts of yourself— spirit, mind, and body.

That weekly time with Erwin helped shift my perspective on self-care completely. I no longer see it as indulgent. I see it as *essential*. I've had some of my most reflective conversations in that chair. Some of my clearest thoughts and some of the best coaching I've ever received was from listening to a man who lives what he speaks and makes people better with his craft.

The shop has become a place of real talk, real connection, and real self-respect. Showing up week after week is one of the strongest things I do for my leadership, my mindset, and my energy.

So yes, my haircut is self-care, but it's not just about the cut—it's about honoring myself.

It's about reminding myself that I matter, that I'm worth the time, and that how I present myself reflects how I feel about my mission.

It's about being *intentional*.

That's the whole point of self-care—it's not about escape, it's about alignment.

For years, I ignored this side of the equation. I would show up for everyone else, but not myself, and I paid for it. I felt stretched thin, disconnected, and worn out. When I started respecting these small rituals—like my haircut—I began to respect myself at a deeper level. That confidence rippled out into every area of my life.

Leadership starts with you. If you can't lead yourself, how can you expect to lead anyone else?

That's why I've remained consistent. It's not vanity, it's *vision*. It's understanding that what seems small becomes significant when it's done with intention. My haircut is a small gesture that made a big impact and it taught me that self-care isn't a break from the mission, it's *part* of the mission.

Every time I leave that shop, I feel sharper, clearer, and more grounded. I'm ready to show up again because I took the time to check in with myself.

SELF-CARE ISN'T THE OPPOSITE OF DRIVE—IT'S THE FUEL

Look at elite athletes, CEOs, and military leaders. They don't just train hard, they recover hard.

They know performance is a cycle: Stress → Recovery → Growth.

Skip the recovery, and you break the system. Skip the self-care, and you become a liability to the mission.

If you want longevity—not just flashes of greatness—you have to lead yourself in the quiet moments, not just the loud ones. Sometimes, the most courageous thing you can do is stop to rest, reflect, and realign.

The world doesn't need more burnt-out leaders who collapse behind the scenes while holding it together in public. The world needs leaders who are whole, grounded, and energized because they've taken the time to care for themselves as much as they care for the mission.

FINAL THOUGHT

Taking care of yourself isn't a luxury—it's leadership.

It's not about checking out, it's about checking in, so you can stay checked in to what matters most.

When you care for yourself with discipline and intention, you don't just feel better—you lead better.

Self-care isn't selfish, it's strategic. It's not soft, it's strong. It's not optional, it's foundational.

Protect your energy like your life depends on it because in leadership, it does.

You can't pour into others if you're running on empty. Refill, refocus, and return stronger.

ACTION STEP

Audit your energy. What's one habit you've been neglecting that would immediately improve your clarity or recovery? Commit to it tonight and protect it like your life depends on it because in a way, it does.

REFLECTION QUESTION

Where in your life are you grinding without refueling and how is that impacting the people who count on your leadership?

Make the space and hold the line. You're not being selfish, you're building strength that lasts.

DECISION-MAKING
THE ART OF CHOOSING WISELY

Decision-making isn't just about picking between options, it's about shaping your future with every choice you make.

Every single day, you're faced with hundreds of decisions. From the simple "what should I eat for breakfast?" to the heavier "should I take this risk in my business or career?" The sum of those choices becomes your reality. Your health, your habits, your career, your relationships, they're all the result of decisions you made in the past.

Here's the truth most people overlook—effective decision-making isn't about knowing the future. It's about trusting yourself to choose, to learn, and to adapt along the way. Leadership demands decisions because the alternative is stagnation. The cost of indecision is often higher than the price of a wrong move.

WHY DECISION-MAKING IS A CORE LEADERSHIP SKILL

Leaders are Decision-Makers

Leadership isn't about waiting for the perfect moment to act, it's about being decisive in the face of uncertainty and guiding others through ambiguity. When you hesitate too long, opportunities pass you by. Bold moves rarely feel perfect in the moment, but leadership lives in action, not in delay.

The Cost of Indecision is High

Indecision drains energy. Whether it's stalling on a promotion opportunity, avoiding a hard conversation, or not addressing an issue with your team—inaction is still a decision. It wastes time, breeds anxiety, and leaves you stuck in neutral. In the leadership world, standing still is moving backward.

Small Decisions Add Up

Think about the last time you skipped a workout. No big deal, right? That one choice often turns into three and then ten missed workouts. The same goes for putting off that important meeting or that difficult phone call. These seemingly minor choices compound. Success isn't one big leap, it's the result of small, consistent, aligned decisions made over time.

HOW TO MAKE BETTER DECISIONS: A LEADERSHIP FRAMEWORK

Clarify Your Values

Every decision should be filtered through the lens of your values. What aligns with your mission, your vision, and your integrity? If you're clear on your values, the decision-making process becomes less about "what if" and more about "what matters most."

Trust Your Gut—Then Validate with Logic

Gut feelings aren't magic, but they are powerful. Your subconscious mind has been collecting data from years of experiences. Trust it, then bring in logic to analyze, validate, and solidify the call. The best decisions blend instinct with intellect.

Embrace the 80/20 Rule

You're never going to have 100% certainty. If you wait for perfect clarity, you'll be stuck forever. Aim for 80% confidence. Make the call, execute, and then pivot if needed. Progress beats perfection every single time.

Learn from Mistakes

Not every decision will work out and that's okay. The most effective leaders aren't the ones who always choose correctly, they're the ones who reflect, adapt, and grow after every move. Mistakes aren't failure —they're feedback.

PERSONAL STORY: THE RAIN, THE CALL, AND THE DECISION THAT DEFINED OUR BRAND

It was February 2024—cold, windy, and pouring rain.

We had been planning one of our first ever A.C.E. outdoor workout events for months. We had twenty seven tickets sold. Momentum was building, excitement was high, but as the date approached, the weather forecast dropped like a weight—cold, windy, and rainy.

It wasn't ideal, it wasn't inspiring, and it definitely wasn't the kind of day people dream of sweating it out outside.

Everyone expected us to cancel and honestly? Part of me did too, until I had a conversation that changed everything.

Sean Degnan and I hopped on a call. It wasn't about logistics first—it was about *leadership.*

We asked one question: *Can we keep people safe?*

Once we confirmed that safety wasn't at risk—our DJ had a tent, the food could be moved indoors, and the setup could hold up—we stopped dancing around it.

We made the decision not to delay, not to half-show up, but to go all in.

Here's what most people miss—anyone can show up when it's sunny and seventy degrees.

Leaders show up when it's raining and thirty seven degrees with wind blowing sideways and every excuse begging them to quit.

We went through with the workout, and sure, seven people didn't end up coming. The twenty people who did, though? They showed up different and they *felt* different.

We weren't just training bodies that day, we were building resilience.

The content we captured was raw, real, and powerful. It wasn't filtered perfection, it was community in the trenches, doing hard things together.

That moment—that cold, wet, muddy moment—became a defining decision for A.C.E.

We took what was supposed to be a one-off outdoor event, and branded a movement—*Outdoor Resilience Training* (ORT).

We weren't just running co-ed workouts.

We were building leaders through discomfort and community through challenge.

We didn't let the environment shape us.

We made a decision and shaped the future of our brand.

Here's the lesson—the decision was a hard one but it became one of our best.

THE IMPACT OF QUICK, CONFIDENT DECISIONS

Being decisive doesn't mean being impulsive and it doesn't mean charging forward without thought. It means being able to cut through the noise, assess what matters, and commit to a direction.

When you decide quickly and confidently, it:

- Builds trust among your team.
- Creates clarity in chaos.
- Drives momentum when things feel stuck.
- Reduces stress by ending the endless loops of doubt and second-guessing.

A leader who dithers creates *confusion*.

A leader who decides creates *confidence*.

FINAL THOUGHT

The act of making decisions is empowering.

It's not about having all the answers, it's about having the courage to act in the face of uncertainty and the humility to learn as you go.

Decisions shape your destiny.

You don't need to know the whole path. You just need to trust yourself enough to take the next step. Today, you can choose to step into the leader you've always been capable of becoming by making one aligned, confident choice.

ACTION STEP

Think about one decision you've been avoiding. Whether it's a tough conversation or an opportunity you're hesitant to seize—take one step today toward making that decision. Once you decide, act with clarity and confidence. *You have the power.*

REFLECTION QUESTION

What's one decision I've been postponing and what would my future-self thank me for choosing today?

LESSON 15
FOCUS
THE POWER OF SINGLE-MINDEDNESS

In a world full of distractions, focus has become one of the most valuable, yet rare, skills a leader can develop. Focus isn't just about narrowing your attention it's about making conscious choices about what deserves your energy, your presence, and your pursuit.

Every day, everything competes for your attention—social media notifications, endless emails, family obligations, late-night hustle culture, and the pressure to always be accessible. In leadership, distractions don't just slow you down, they derail your ability to make impact.

Focus is your ability to lock in on what matters most, to build a fortress around your priorities, and to say "no" more often than you say "yes."

WHY FOCUS IS ESSENTIAL FOR SUCCESS

Focus Leads to Mastery

You can't master anything if your attention is split in a dozen directions. Whether you're trying to grow a business, strengthen a relationship, or lead a team, success demands deep, concentrated effort.

Shallow focus gets shallow results. Mastery is only possible when you go all in, one task at a time.

Focus Drives Results

High performers don't get more time than anyone else. They just protect their time and attention more fiercely. Focus is a force multiplier. You get more done, at a higher level, in less time because you're not chasing every shiny object.

Focus Creates Clarity

The more distractions you eliminate, the clearer your thinking becomes. When you focus deeply, patterns emerge. Solutions become visible, opportunities reveal themselves, and decision-making becomes faster and sharper.

HOW TO IMPROVE FOCUS: A LEADERSHIP STRATEGY

Prioritize Your Day

Start each morning by identifying your top three priorities. What must get done today for the day to be considered a win? Align your schedule with those. Anything outside of those is either noise or can wait.

Use the Pomodoro Technique

Work in focused intervals of twenty-five to thirty minutes, followed by short breaks. These bursts of productivity keep your mind sharp and prevent burnout. You train your brain to focus, and it becomes second nature.

Eliminate Distractions

Silence your phone, turn off notifications, and use website blockers. Create a workspace that supports focus, set boundaries with people who constantly interrupt your flow, and be ruthless about protecting your mental space.

Focus on One Thing at a Time

Multitasking is a myth since your brain can only give full attention to one thing at a time. When you switch tasks, you lose momentum. Commit to finishing what you start. Momentum builds when attention is undivided.

Practice Deep Work

Schedule blocks of time each day for uninterrupted, high-impact work. No meetings, no emails, no messages—just you and the mission. These deep work sessions are where transformation happens.

Create a Focus Ritual

A ritual signals to your brain that it's time to concentrate. This could be lighting a candle, putting on headphones, or even making a cup of coffee before diving in. Over time, this simple ritual becomes a mental trigger for flow.

Audit Your Energy

Your ability to focus is deeply tied to your physical and emotional energy. Get sleep, stay hydrated, and fuel your body with quality nutrition. When your body is run-down, your brain follows.

PERSONAL STORY: THE NIGHT I CHOSE PEACE OVER HUSTLE

For the first decade of my career, I thought being available twenty-four hours per day, seven days per week was a badge of honor. I lived in constant connection—responding to DMs, checking email at midnight, taking client calls late at night. My phone was always buzzing. It felt like I was grinding and in some ways, I was.

It came at a cost though.

It led to fights in past relationships because my focus was constantly divided. I couldn't be fully present with loved ones, especially in the evenings. I was anxious, overstimulated, and my sleep suffered for years. I was physically exhausted but mentally wired.

The worst part? I thought this was what leaders were supposed to do.

Then I made a decision that changed my leadership, my presence, and my peace—I set my phone to "Do Not Disturb" every night at 9 PM.

Simple but it was revolutionary.

Was it easy? *No.*

I worried about missing out and I probably lost a few bucks here and there, but what I gained was far greater—peace, clarity, and intentional presence. My evenings became sacred, I could wind down properly, and I reflected more. My sleep improved but more importantly, I became fully present for the most important person in my life, my daughter, Kali.

Instead of scrolling or stressing about business, I read to her, I sang worship music with her, I tucked her in, and I watched her fall asleep. These became some of the most meaningful moments of my day.

Focus gave me the ability to shift from just building business to building memories, building legacy, and building a bond with my daughter that can't be bought.

Here's the thing—hustle culture doesn't teach you this. They'll have you believe that every second counts only if it's tied to a paycheck. Some moments are more valuable than money though, because they'll shape how you're remembered.

That small decision—*Do Not Disturb at 9 PM*—wasn't about avoiding work, it was about choosing to lead with presence. To choose peace over pressure—to stop reacting and start living intentionally.

Ironically, by focusing more on my family, my business improved too. I showed up the next day more grounded, more creative, and more resilient. That's the paradox of focus—when you protect what matters most, everything else starts to thrive too.

THE TRUE POWER OF FOCUS

Focus isn't just about productivity, it's about intentional living.

When you focus, you sharpen your edge. You're not scattered, you're not reactive, you're locked in. Present and purposefully.

Think of your focus like a laser beam cutting through the chaos of life to illuminate what actually matters. That level of attention makes you magnetic and it attracts results, people, and peace.

As a leader, your focus sets the tone. If you're scattered, so is your team, but if you're locked in, they mirror that. You become a standard of calm in a world of noise.

FINAL THOUGHT

Focus is a leadership superpower. It's not something you're born with —it's something you train.

Here's the truth—every time you say yes to a distraction, you say no to your goals.

Your focus is your future. If you want to move faster, go further, and lead more powerfully, protect your attention like your life depends on it, *because it does*.

ACTION STEP

Identify the biggest distraction in your day whether it's your phone, social media, or an old habit that drains your energy. Eliminate it for the next hour. Put your phone away, turn off the noise, and lock in on one meaningful task. When you focus, you'll be amazed at what you're truly capable of.

REFLECTION QUESTION

Where in your life are you trading long-term fulfillment for short-term stimulation?

What one decision could help you focus on what truly matters?

BUILDING TRUST
THE BRIDGE BETWEEN LEADERS AND TEAMS

Trust isn't something you can demand, it's something you must earn.

It's not granted by title, seniority, or your years of experience. It's built in moments of consistency, proven through integrity, and tested when things don't go according to plan.

Trust is the bedrock of leadership.

Without it, you have nothing. With it, you can lead anyone, anywhere.

Whether you're in the boardroom, on the shop floor, or standing in your living room trying to lead your family through another tough season—trust is the glue that holds it all together. No strategy, vision, or system can replace the power of trust.

WHY TRUST IS THE CORNERSTONE OF LEADERSHIP

Trust Accelerates Decision-Making

When your team trusts you, they don't second-guess your guidance. You eliminate hesitation. They know that even if it's not perfect, your intentions are aligned with what's best for the mission and for them. Trust lets you move with speed and clarity which is critical in today's fast-moving business landscape.

Trust Fosters Collaboration

When people trust each other, they speak up. They share ideas, challenge assumptions, and contribute without fear. In environments where trust runs deep, innovation flourishes because there's safety even in the perceived face of failure. Google's *Project Aristotle* found that the most effective teams weren't those with the highest IQs or skillsets, they were the ones with the highest levels of *psychological safety*, a byproduct of deep trust.

Trust Keeps Teams Cohesive

In hard times, it's trust that holds people together. Without trust, adversity breaks a team apart. With trust, they become tighter, more resilient, and more committed than ever. During crisis, trust is the difference between retreat and rally.

HOW TO BUILD TRUST AS A LEADER

Be Transparent

Leaders don't have to know everything but they do have to be honest. When things go wrong, own it. When plans change, explain why. Transparency earns respect, and respect fuels trust. Silence and secrecy break connection.

Follow Through on Your Promises

If you say it, do it. Don't cancel one-on-ones and don't push off commitments. Even in the smallest details, consistency builds credibility. When people know your word means something, they'll trust it. Warren Buffett put it simply, *"It takes twenty years to build a reputation and five minutes to ruin it."*

Show Vulnerability

It's not weakness, it's humanity. When you admit mistakes or ask for help, you create connection. Vulnerability disarms defensiveness and makes people want to follow you because they see you're real—it breeds loyalty, not pity.

Lead with Integrity

Do the right thing, even when no one's watching. People pay more attention to how you act when it's hard. That's when character is revealed and trust is either solidified or shattered.

Be Consistent

Your team shouldn't have to guess who you are today. When your behavior is stable, people feel secure. They don't have to worry about emotional shifts or favoritism, and can focus on the mission, not your mood.

A PERSONAL STORY: WHEN TRUST LAUNCHED MY VOICE

I'll never forget that summer day in Elmsford, New York. I was early in my leadership career, working in local government, still learning how to walk in the shoes of a leader. I was lucky to be surrounded by people who saw more in me than I saw in myself.

Commissioner Andre Early and Deputy Commissioner Terrance Jackson were my guides—seasoned leaders, respected voices, men who moved with confidence and poise. On this day, they invited me to join them for a community visit at Liberty Coca-Cola to share some of the positive impact we were making in Greenburgh and to explore partnership opportunities.

Normally, I played my part behind the scenes—working the floor, shaking hands, building relationships. Public speaking? That wasn't in the job description, at least not for me.

Just moments before they were set to deliver remarks to the crowd of about one hundred and fifty people—which might as well have been fifteen thousand to me—they tapped me on the shoulder.

"Now's your chance," they said.

I froze for a moment. "Wait, me?"

They nodded. No notes, no preparation—just *belief*.

They trusted me.

They believed I had the knowledge, the presence, and the heart to speak on behalf of our department and on behalf of the mission we lived for every day. So, I stepped up. Nervous? Absolutely, but I delivered.

In that moment, something changed in me.

That trust, that belief, and that empowerment, sparked a flame I didn't know was there. It was humbling and exhilarating all at once. It became the start of my journey into public speaking, a gift I now use in every corner of my leadership.

To this day, I pay that trust forward. When I see someone on my team who's ready—even if they don't know it yet—I nudge them forward. I give them a shot and I trust them.

Sometimes the most powerful thing you can do as a leader is believe in someone before they believe in themselves.

TRUST IN ACTION: BUSINESS AND ATHLETIC GREATNESS

Let's talk business. One of the most remarkable examples of trust creating an unstoppable culture is Satya Nadella's leadership at Microsoft.

When Nadella became CEO in 2014, Microsoft was seen as bureaucratic and stagnant. One of his first moves wasn't strategic, it was cultural. He focused on rebuilding internal trust, he encouraged vulnerability, he asked senior leaders to adopt a growth mindset, and he emphasized empathy as a business skill.

Under his leadership, trust became the language of Microsoft. Teams were empowered and innovation returned. In just five years, Microsoft's market cap tripled, not because of a product shift, but because trust rebuilt the foundation.

In sports, consider Steph Curry. He's not the loudest voice in the locker room, but ask anyone around him—the Warriors are Steph's team because his consistency and humility earned deep trust. He doesn't need to dominate every play. Quite simply, his presence creates *space*. Teammates trust he'll hit the shot, but more importantly they trust he'll pass it if it's the right play. That trust led to four NBA championships and one of the most unselfish dynasties in league history.

Trust scales and turns good teams into great ones.

THE RIPPLE EFFECT OF TRUST

Trust doesn't stay in one place, it multiplies.

When you build trust with your team, you create a ripple. People start trusting each other more, they open up, they collaborate, and they have each other's backs. It becomes cultural.

Here's the kicker—trust isn't just a "soft skill"—it's a *hard* advantage. Teams that trust one another outperform those that don't. Period.

A 2017 Harvard Business Review study showed that employees at high-trust companies report 74% less stress, 106% more energy at work, and 50% higher productivity.

Trust in leadership is one of the top predictors of employee engagement and retention.

Trust increases speed, reduces turnover, improves morale, and strengthens your bottom line.

Never forget—trust takes time to build and seconds to break—it's not a one-time effort, it's an everyday investment.

FINAL THOUGHT

You may hold the title, you may have the authority, but if you don't have trust, you're not leading—you're just managing.

True leadership is built on influence and influence is earned through trust.

The great paradox? The more trust you give, the more power you gain—not over people, but with them. That's the kind of leadership that lasts.

Earn it, protect it, and use it to elevate everyone around you.

ACTION STEP

Identify one person or group in your life—your team, your partner, your child—where trust could be strengthened.

Take one tangible step today to reinforce it. Be honest, keep a promise, admit a mistake, and lead with integrity. One action, done right, can change the entire dynamic.

REFLECTION QUESTION

When was the last time someone put their trust in you and how did it impact belief in yourself?

More importantly, who's waiting on you to do the same for them?

VISION
THE COMPASS OF LEADERSHIP

A leader without a vision is like a ship without a rudder—drifting aimlessly, vulnerable to the tides and winds of life. Vision is the ability to see what others cannot, to define a compelling future, and to inspire others to work toward it.

Vision doesn't show up fully formed. It begins as a whisper, a pull in your gut, an idea in the back of your mind, a moment where clarity meets courage. If you listen closely, that whisper can grow into a movement.

A vision is not just about setting goals or dreaming big, it's about *seeing* what could be, even when the current reality says otherwise. It's about anchoring yourself in a belief so strong, it can't be shaken by today's storms. It's about building a path for others to walk with you, not just behind you.

Vision isn't extra—it's essential, especially in leadership.

WHY VISION IS ESSENTIAL FOR LEADERSHIP

Vision Provides Direction

Without a clear vision, leadership becomes a reaction to problems rather than a pursuit of purpose. With it, you lead *on offense*. You don't just respond to the world, you shape it.

Vision Fuels Motivation

On the days when things fall apart, when the team doubts the mission, when you're stretched thin, vision is the fuel. It reminds you *why* you started and when shared effectively, it becomes a powerful engine for others too.

Vision Aligns Your Team

When your team knows the destination, they can row in rhythm. No more wasted energy. Vision creates unity. It gives meaning to the mundane and lifts small tasks into significant contributions.

HOW TO CREATE AND COMMUNICATE YOUR VISION

Define Your "Why"

Before vision becomes a direction, it must come from conviction. Why does your vision matter? What makes it non-negotiable to you? Dig deep and get honest—this is the root system that keeps your leadership grounded.

Make It Inspiring

Your vision should make people sit up and stir emotion inside of them. You're not writing a to-do list, you're painting a picture of a better future. Make it bold, make it emotional, and make it *unforgettable*.

Be Specific but Flexible

The goal must be clear, but the route can shift. Think like GPS—the destination doesn't change, but if there's traffic, it'll reroute you. Don't fall in love with the plan, fall in love with the *purpose*.

Communicate Consistently

Vision fades fast if it's only spoken once. It must become part of your language, your meetings, your culture. People need to *hear it, see it, and feel it*. Over-communicate until it becomes contagious.

Involve Others

People buy into what they help build. When your team feels like co-authors of the vision, they become emotionally invested. Ask questions, take feedback, and build *with* them, not just *for* them.

THE POWER OF VISION IN ACTION: MY PERSONAL STORY

I spent years building my leadership career—establishing my name in local government, climbing the ranks, and finding my voice in boardrooms and community meetings. Behind that public journey was a parallel, quieter one—rebuilding my body, my confidence, and my health through fitness.

I've battled Crohn's disease since I was a kid. It's not glamorous. It meant carrying toilet paper in my backpack in high school. It meant fatigue, flare-ups, and fear but I didn't quit. I trained, I ate better, and I rebuilt my body brick by brick.

Still, I carried doubt. I'd look in the mirror and see strength, but I'd hesitate to claim my worth. I was working with companies like Orgain and ProLon—unpaid partnerships, free products in exchange for posts. It was good but not aligned with the vision I had for myself.

One day, I found clarity. I told a few trusted friends first, "I've worked seventeen years to build this body, this brand, this message—and I'm done settling for free product. I want to be paid. I want a five-figure brand deal. I want to represent companies that *align* with who I am and what I stand for."

Then I said it publicly and I shared it on social media. It wasn't cocky, it was *conviction*. When the vision became clear, opportunity followed.

Within weeks, four companies reached out. I ended up signing with a major supplement brand that was profiting $250,000 in monthly revenue. They were happy to offer me the compensation I requested.

That partnership wasn't just a paycheck—it was proof. Proof that when you *own your vision*, the world begins to match your energy. When you *declare what you're building*, people come to support or step aside.

VISION IN THE REAL WORLD

Think about Walt Disney. When he envisioned Disneyland, everyone thought he was delusional. A theme park based on animated characters? "A waste of money," they said. But Walt had a vision, not just of rides but of *imagination brought to life*. He saw it so clearly, he could describe the streets, the sounds, the energy. Today, the Disney brand is worth over $150 billion and it all started with a man who dared to imagine something that didn't exist.

Howard Schultz envisioned Starbucks not just as a coffee shop, but as a "third place" between home and work, a community hub. That vision transformed a small Seattle coffee bean store into a global empire. Not because of coffee but because of *culture* and *connection*.

Serena Williams once said, "I don't like to lose at anything yet I've grown most not from victories, but setbacks." Her vision wasn't just about Grand Slams—it was about redefining what power, femininity, and resilience looked like. That vision carried her through criticism, injury, motherhood, and history-making moments.

Great athletes don't train for trophies, they train for *legacy*. That's the power of vision—it stretches beyond the scoreboard.

FINAL THOUGHT

Vision is what separates the distracted from the driven. It turns talent into transformation and motion into movement.

You don't need all the answers and you don't need permission, you just need clarity and the courage to declare it.

A leader with a vision can ignite a team, shift a culture, and spark a revolution.

ACTION STEP

Write down your vision. Make it bold, clear, and real. Then speak it out loud. Share it with at least one person today—someone who can challenge you and support you. Clarity is the first step, communication is the second, and commitment is the third.

REFLECTION QUESTION

Are you reacting to life or are you leading it?

What vision would make your future worth fighting for?

LESSON 18
COURAGE

THE STRENGTH TO LEAD IN THE FACE OF FEAR

Courage isn't the absence of fear, it's the decision to act in the presence of it. It's standing at the edge of uncertainty and choosing to leap. For leaders, courage is not a luxury—it's a necessity. Without it, progress stalls, teams stagnate, and your potential as a leader never fully ignites.

Every leader, no matter how seasoned, battles fear—fear of failure, fear of rejection, fear of judgment, fear of being misunderstood. What separates average leaders from great ones is not that they feel less fear, it's that they *move anyway*. They speak when it's uncomfortable, act when it's risky, and show up even when their confidence wavers.

Courage is not just heroic action, it's a daily decision. It's the internal tug to lean into what you'd rather run from. Every courageous act—no matter how small—compounds into strength, influence, and credibility over time.

WHY COURAGE IS ESSENTIAL FOR LEADERSHIP

Courage Drives Innovation

No innovation happens in the comfort zone. Every breakthrough, every bold idea, every revolutionary solution requires stepping into the unknown. Courage is the foundation for thinking differently, challenging norms, and trying again after failure. Leaders who innovate do so not because they're fearless, but because they choose boldness over safety.

Courage Enables Decision-Making

Leadership demands hard decisions—firing someone, ending a partnership, pivoting your strategy, saying "no" when everyone else expects a "yes." The weight of leadership is real, but courage enables you to carry it with clarity. You don't always get certainty, but with courage, you get conviction—and that's often what's needed most.

Courage Inspires Others to Act

People aren't inspired by perfection, they're inspired by boldness. When you lead with courage, you give others permission to do the same. You normalize discomfort. You make vulnerability safe. You become proof that it's okay to take risks—and that even if you fall, you can rise.

Courage Builds Resilience

You will fail. That's not a possibility, it's a guarantee. But courage isn't just about charging into battle, it's about getting up after the loss. Courage gives you the grit to keep going, to try again, and to carry lessons forward. Every setback becomes a stepping stone when courage is part of your foundation.

HOW TO CULTIVATE COURAGE AS A LEADER

Acknowledge Your Fear

Fear becomes dangerous when ignored. Call it out, write it down, and say it aloud. You take its power away when you name it. By acknowledging fear, you also remind yourself that it's a natural part of growth, not a sign you're broken or incapable.

Take Small Risks First

You don't build courage overnight. Like a muscle, it strengthens with reps. Start small, initiate a tough conversation, set a boundary, and ask for help. Each small courageous act builds your tolerance for bigger challenges.

Visualize Success

Most of us play out worst-case scenarios in our heads. What if instead you visualized the *best-case*? See yourself delivering the keynote. Picture your team thriving after a tough decision. Rehearsing success in your mind builds familiarity and reduces the fear tied to unfamiliar outcomes.

Surround Yourself with Support

Courage isn't a solo sport. When you're surrounded by people who believe in you, who reflect your strength when you forget it, fear shrinks. Choose mentors, friends, and teammates who encourage boldness and lean on them when courage feels scarce.

Learn from Failure

Courageous leaders don't see failure as final. They see it as feedback. The most transformational growth often comes on the other side of falling flat. Reflect, recalibrate, and rise. Every stumble becomes part of your leadership story if you have the courage to own it.

PERSONAL STORY: THE MOMENT I CHOSE TO LEAD WITH COURAGE

There's one moment that comes to mind every time I think about courage and it wasn't on a stage, in front of a crowd, or during some high-stakes business deal. It was on a podcast.

Early in my podcasting days, I was invited as a guest to speak on leadership and personal growth. The conversation was going well, until the host asked a question that tugged at something deep in me. It wasn't scripted and it wasn't planned, but suddenly, I felt the urge to speak a truth I had buried for years.

I had never publicly talked about a major mistake from my past—infidelity in a previous relationship. It was something I had long been ashamed of, something that haunted me quietly even though I had spent years growing from it. At the time, I still carried the identity of that mistake, even though my actions, values, and life had changed.

In that moment, there was a war in my mind. Part of me screamed to keep quiet, *"Don't say it. People will judge you. They'll think less of you. They won't see you the same."* But another part of me—the leader I had been working to become—knew the truth. If I wanted to lead with authenticity, I had to start here, and I had to stop hiding.

So, I said it. I spoke openly about my past, the shame I had carried, and the lessons I had learned from making one of the biggest mistakes of my life. I didn't glamorize it, I didn't justify it, I owned it.

The response? It changed everything.

That episode became one of the most powerful conversations I've ever had. People reached out thanking me for the honesty, for giving them permission to stop hiding from their own shame. Men who were struggling in silence, women who had felt betrayed, and leaders who thought they had to pretend to be perfect—all found strength in that moment of courage.

I realized something important that day. **We are not defined by our mistakes—we're defined by the courageous choices we make after them.**

Wearing my past on my sleeve wasn't weakness, it was credibility. People don't just want to know your wins, they want to know your journey. If we aren't willing to share where we've been, we rob others of the belief that change is possible, especially as leaders.

If we pretend we've always had it all together, we make growth look unattainable.

Courage isn't about being perfect, it's about being *real*. That podcast didn't just help others, it freed me. It reminded me that leadership is about honesty, vulnerability, and showing others what it looks like to stand tall in your truth.

FINAL THOUGHT

Courage is the silent force behind every bold step in leadership. It's the fuel that powers truth, growth, risk, and recovery. Without courage, you may still lead—but you'll always hold back the part of you that could've changed someone's life.

It's not easy to confront fear and it's not easy to share your flaws, but when you do, something powerful happens—people start believing they can do it too.

Let this be the reminder—*you don't have to be fearless to lead.* You just have to be brave enough to take the next right step, even when your voice shakes.

ACTION STEP

What's one truth you've been afraid to share, one conversation you've been avoiding, or one decision fear has kept you from making?

Choose one. Take one small courageous action today and either send the message, ask the question, or make the choice.

Remember— courage isn't about doing it all, it's about doing the next thing that matters most.

REFLECTION QUESTION

Where in your life or leadership are you currently letting fear lead, and what courageous conversation, action, or truth are you avoiding that could set you free?

DISCOMFORT
THE KEY TO GROWTH AND TRANSFORMATION

Discomfort is often misunderstood. We're taught to run from it and we're conditioned to believe that if something feels uncomfortable, it's probably wrong. But here's the truth, comfort rarely breeds greatness. Discomfort is not the enemy, it's the compass.

As Tony Robbins says, "All growth starts at the end of your comfort zone." If that's true—and it is—then discomfort is the signal that you're on the edge of your next breakthrough. In leadership, it's not just a personal signal, it's a professional imperative.

WHY THIS LESSON MATTERS IN LEADERSHIP

You don't grow by repeating what's easy. You grow when you do the hard things like having the tough conversations, making the unpopular decisions, staying late when you're exhausted, saying no when everyone expects a yes, and standing firm when it would be easier to fold. Growth happens when you're uncomfortable. Period.

In a 2023 Harvard Business Review study on effective leadership traits, "comfort with discomfort" ranked as one of the top five differentiators of high-performing executives. The same study found that leaders who actively sought discomfort in learning and decision-making environments were 31% more likely to lead teams that exceeded performance benchmarks. The data is clear—avoiding discomfort limits your leadership while embracing discomfort transforms it.

WHY DISCOMFORT IS ESSENTIAL FOR LEADERSHIP

Discomfort Breeds Resilience

Leaders are forged in fire, not born. Every challenge you face, every obstacle you overcome, adds a layer to your character. Discomfort builds the grit that leadership requires.

Whether it's navigating a financial downturn, confronting a toxic culture, or simply choosing to keep going when it would be easier to quit—discomfort trains your resilience muscle. You don't get tougher by avoiding struggle, you get tougher by walking through it.

Discomfort Fosters Learning

Let's get real—if you only do what you're good at, you'll never get better. Discomfort is a signal that you're learning something new. It means you're growing beyond what you already know and what you already are.

Whether it's public speaking, giving performance feedback, or stepping into a room full of people more experienced than you—leaning into those moments is how you transform from capable to exceptional.

Discomfort Accelerates Innovation

Innovation does not live in your comfort zone. It lives in the unknown —where there's risk, uncertainty, and potential failure. Great leaders ask the hard questions, "What if we tried something different?" or "What's not working here, and why are we still doing it?"

Discomfort forces creativity. It pushes you to think differently, to solve problems rather than just manage them. A McKinsey report found that teams led by leaders who encouraged discomfort-driven innovation were 45% more likely to pioneer successful new initiatives within their first year.

Discomfort Sharpens Decision-Making

Discomfort also plays a major role in clarity. When you're forced to make a call in the middle of pressure and uncertainty, you grow in your ability to lead with conviction. Leaders who learn to make hard decisions, even when it's uncomfortable, build trust, respect, and authority.

Avoiding discomfort often leads to decision paralysis. Embracing it leads to decisiveness—and decisiveness is a hallmark of great leadership.

HOW TO LEAN INTO DISCOMFORT AS A LEADER

Shift Your Mindset About Discomfort

Stop seeing discomfort as a red flag and start seeing it as a green light. Reframe your thinking. Instead of saying, "This is hard," say, "This is the work." Instead of saying, "I'm nervous," say, "I'm stretching." The discomfort you feel is not a barrier, it's evidence that you're evolving.

Tony Robbins often says, "If you're not growing, you're dying." That's not dramatic. It's accurate. If your leadership feels too comfortable, you're likely stagnant. Shift your mindset. Seek challenge. Seek growth.

Take Small Risks Regularly

You don't need to leap off cliffs to grow. Start small, speak up in a meeting, tackle a project outside your comfort zone, or address the minor conflict you've been avoiding. Like weightlifting, every small rep of discomfort builds your tolerance for bigger challenges. Don't wait for the massive moment, train for it every day.

Develop Mental Toughness

Mental toughness is your ability to be calm, clear, and committed even when things get tough. Discomfort is its training ground. When pressure rises, train yourself to breathe, think, act—not react. Learn to get comfortable being uncomfortable. That's the edge that separates leaders who last from those who burn out.

Surround Yourself with Truth-Tellers

Discomfort is easier to navigate when you're not alone. Surround yourself with people who will tell you the truth, push you forward, and support your journey. Seek coaches, mentors, and colleagues who understand that growth requires friction and who aren't afraid to challenge you when necessary.

Learn from Every Discomfort

Every uncomfortable situation holds a lesson. After the challenge passes, don't just move on—debrief. Ask yourself: "What did I learn? What worked? What could I do differently next time?" Leadership isn't just about moving forward, it's about extracting wisdom from the moments that test you.

MY STORY: THE NIGHT I LOST MY BEST FRIEND—AND FOUND A BREAKTHROUGH

His name was Chance.

I got him as a six-week-old Pitbull puppy while I was in college—young, broke, and reckless enough to sneak him into my dorm room. I named him "Chance" because everyone told me not to get a pit. They were "dangerous, aggressive, and not to be trusted." I've never been one to follow the crowd, though. I believed he deserved a chance and truthfully, I think I needed one too.

We were inseparable. I got kicked out of my first apartment for trying to hide him in a no-dog building that only allowed cats. I didn't care because I had my best friend. Most people wait until their dog passes to get a tattoo but not me. I had his portrait inked on my chest after just two years—that's how deep the bond was.

Chance saw me through my lowest seasons when I was drinking too much, making poor decisions, and trying to figure out who I was. He never judged me, he just stayed close, loyal, and present. He was quiet strength.

In 2019, we moved into a home together, the first one with a back-yard and his own little entrance. It felt like a win we earned side by side. He had food allergies and aging joints, but I kept him on a special diet and meds, just doing what I could to keep him happy and healthy.

Then in 2020, my daughter Kali Michelle was born. Chance became her protector overnight. He'd growl if someone got too close. If she cried, he barked until someone showed up to help. It was like he instinctively knew his new role. She was his sister now.

In 2022, life changed again—my marriage ended. A house that once felt full suddenly felt hollow. There were nights I'd cry quietly on the couch, or wake up from nightmares and sneak into the living room just to breathe. Every time—and I mean every time—Chance was there. Even if I didn't call him, even if I tried not to wake him, he just knew. Curling up beside me until I drifted back to sleep, he obviously couldn't speak words but his presence was felt beyond any verbal forms of comfort.

Eventually, his health started to fail. His legs gave out more often, his energy dropped, and eventually, I had to make the most painful decision I've ever made. *I let him go.*

On April 13, 2023, at 2:40 PM, I held my best friend as a vet came to our home and put him to sleep peacefully. My father and brother were by my side while worship music played in the background. I kissed his face and thanked him for the years he spent with me, filled with laughter, protection, loyalty, and unconditional love. We locked eyes one final time and I whispered a prayer—that he would go in peace, and that somehow, I would find peace too.

That night, something unexpected happened.

I slept.

For the first time in months, I had a full, uninterrupted night of sleep. It didn't make logical sense. I had just lost my greatest comfort. My house was *truly* empty now but facing grief head-on cracked something open inside me. That night marked a turning point—not just in my healing, but in my leadership.

THE POWER OF DISCOMFORT IN LEADERSHIP

Here's the truth—most leaders won't have the courage to lean into discomfort and that's exactly why most won't grow past a certain point. The ones who embrace the tough conversations, face the friction, and choose principle over popularity—those are the ones who create real impact.

Discomfort will either break you down or break you open—and sometimes the only way out is through. I thought the sleepless nights would last forever. But when I confronted the pain instead of avoiding it, when I surrendered to the discomfort instead of numbing it—there was peace on the other side. A new level of calm, of trust in myself, and of strength.

That's the thing about discomfort, it doesn't always make sense in the moment. It just hurts. But leadership—real leadership—is built in those silent, sacred, and uncomfortable spaces. If you feel uncomfortable right now in your role, your business, or your life, that's a good thing. It means you're alive, it means you're growing, and it means you're leading.

You might not be putting down a dog but maybe you're letting go of a relationship, a position, a business plan, or a version of yourself that no longer fits. It's terrifying but if you walk through the pain, not around it, breakthrough is on the other side.

The night I said goodbye to Chance, I also said goodbye to fear, to unrest, and to the version of me that couldn't sleep without comfort. I haven't struggled since.

Sometimes, the only way to level up, is to lose something you thought you couldn't live without.

FINAL THOUGHT

Growth is not supposed to feel safe. It's supposed to feel uncertain, awkward, and sometimes even lonely. But on the other side of that discomfort is power. The kind of power that can't be handed to you, only earned through experience.

Don't numb it, don't avoid it, and don't hide from it. Walk straight into it with discipline, with courage, and with the knowledge that discomfort is not your enemy—it's your edge.

ACTION STEP

Discomfort often reveals the exact place where your next breakthrough lives. Today, identify one situation you've been avoiding because it makes you uncomfortable. Don't overthink it, just find one and then write it down.

Now, take one action. Send the message, make the call, schedule the meeting, or push the weight. Take the step.

Lean into the discomfort. That's where your leadership begins.

REFLECTION QUESTION

What area of your life or leadership have you been avoiding because it feels too uncomfortable and what might be possible if you faced it today?

CREATIVITY
UNLOCKING NEW POSSIBILITIES IN LEADERSHIP

Creativity is often viewed as the domain of artists, designers, or musicians. In leadership, creativity isn't about painting a masterpiece or composing a song, it's about seeing possibilities where others see walls, about forging new paths when the old ones no longer serve. Creativity is the engine that drives innovation, adaptability, and resilience—three essentials of effective leadership.

As John Maxwell says, *"Leadership is influence. Everything rises and falls on leadership."* Creativity is the spark that allows leaders to influence in new, powerful ways. It moves beyond conventional thinking and brings fresh solutions to old and new problems alike.

At its core, creativity is problem-solving. Every leader faces obstacles —team conflicts, market shifts, strategic dead ends. A creative leader refuses to settle for easy or familiar answers. They dig deeper, look sideways, and often upend expectations to find solutions no one else sees. Creativity lets you transform challenges into opportunities and stoke momentum when the status quo fails.

WHY CREATIVITY IS ESSENTIAL FOR LEADERSHIP

Creative Leaders Foster Innovation

Innovation isn't just about flashy new gadgets or breakthrough tech, it's about creating better ways to serve, to grow, and to lead. The best leaders don't simply accept "how it's always been," they question, experiment, and push boundaries. Without creativity, leadership stagnates, stuck in cycles of repetition.

Creativity Enhances Adaptability

Change is constant. Markets evolve, teams shift, and crises emerge. Creative leaders don't panic—they pivot and they use creativity as a survival tool—adjusting strategies, communication styles, and operations on the fly. This flexibility is what separates leaders who thrive from those who falter.

Creative Problem-Solving is Key to Overcoming Challenges

When the same old playbook no longer works, creativity rewrites the game. Leaders who rely solely on routine hit walls. Creative leaders step back, reconsider, and find fresh perspectives. They turn constraints into springboards for new ideas.

Creativity Fuels Resilience

Resilience is more than bouncing back, it's bouncing forward and it's using failure as fertilizer for growth. Creative leaders view setbacks as invitations to innovate rather than reasons to quit. Creativity empowers leaders to reimagine what's possible after defeat.

HOW TO CULTIVATE CREATIVITY AS A LEADER

Allow Space for Ideas

Creativity can't flourish under pressure and constant distraction. Leaders must intentionally carve out time to think, reflect, and brainstorm. For me, this was often early mornings or late nights—moments when my mind could wander and ideas could spark. If you never create space for creativity, it won't surprise you with solutions.

Experiment with New Approaches

Creativity demands action. You have to try new leadership styles, communication methods, or problem-solving tactics. Some will fail, but those failures are stepping stones. Embrace them. Experimentation breeds breakthroughs.

Collaborate with Diverse Thinkers

No one has a monopoly on creativity. The best ideas often come from the friction of diverse perspectives. Surround yourself with people who think differently—different backgrounds, experiences, and worldviews. This diversity stirs your own thinking and expands the creative pool.

Challenge Assumptions

Great leaders ask: "Why do we do it this way? What if there's a better way?" They refuse to let "because we've always done it" be the final answer. This simple mindset shift is a gateway to creativity and innovation.

Embrace Failure as Part of the Creative Process

If fear of failure holds you back, your creativity will suffocate. Leaders create cultures where failure is a learning opportunity—not a career-ender. This freedom to fail without judgment is the soil where bold ideas grow.

A PERSONAL STORY: CREATIVITY AT THE NIKEID COUNTER

Years ago, while working at Nike during college, I was stationed at the NikeID counter—a game-changing concept that let customers design and personalize their own sneakers. I looked forward to every shift there because it wasn't just a job, it was a front-row seat to creativity in action.

Helping customers bring their ideas to life was powerful. I saw people pour their identities into their shoes—choosing colors, materials, even custom text—turning a pair of sneakers into a personal statement. It was a unique kind of artistry that wasn't just about aesthetics but about storytelling and self-expression.

The creativity I witnessed at that counter was inspiring—and contagious. I made mock-ups for myself regularly, experimenting with bold colorways and combinations that made me feel like a true visionary. Seeing the iconic Nike swoosh on something I designed felt like owning a piece of the future.

During those shifts, I met incredible people—athletes and artists like John Starks, Jadakiss, Mariano Rivera, and DMX—who were drawn to NikeID's innovative spirit. The platform wasn't just about shoes, it was a cultural movement that celebrated individuality and creativity.

NikeID eventually evolved into "Nike By You," but the essence remains the same—creativity is at the heart of the world's top athletic brand. Nike thrives because it encourages people to think differently, express themselves, and push limits—core principles every leader should embody.

This experience taught me that creativity isn't an abstract concept reserved for artists, it's a practical tool for leadership. Just like customizing a shoe, leadership requires vision, personalization, and bold choices.

THE POWER OF CREATIVITY IN LEADERSHIP

Creative leadership is about vision *and* action. It's not enough to dream of a better future, you must take steps to create it. Creativity lets you see what others don't and lead your team toward new possibilities.

John Maxwell emphasizes that *"A leader is one who knows the way, goes the way, and shows the way."* Creativity equips you to find the way no one else has, to go there boldly, and to bring your team along with confidence.

When you embrace creativity, you don't just solve problems—you transform environments, inspire innovation, encourage risk-taking, and build resilience. Your team feels empowered to challenge norms and bring their own creativity to the table, multiplying the leadership impact.

FINAL THOUGHT

Creativity is not a luxury for leaders, it's a necessity. It expands your influence, deepens your impact, and equips you to lead with vision and courage. Without creativity, leadership is confined to rules and repetition; with creativity, leadership becomes limitless.

As you lead, remember that the world's greatest brands and leaders—from Nike to John Maxwell—thrive on creative thinking. You also have to.

ACTION STEP

Choose a challenge in your life or leadership that feels stuck or repetitive. Instead of defaulting to your usual approach, brainstorm three completely different ways to tackle it—no idea too bold or unconventional. Pick one idea and take immediate action to start making it real.

REFLECTION QUESTION

When was the last time you truly allowed yourself to think differently —beyond the obvious—and how did it change your leadership or results?

What's one area in your life or work where you can challenge the status quo today by tapping into your creative courage?

PART THREE
LEAD TO MULTIPLY

DELEGATION
LETTING GO TO LEAD FORWARD

One of the most misunderstood and underutilized tools in leadership is delegation.

High performers—especially new or ambitious leaders—often fall into the trap of believing that doing it all themselves is the only way to ensure it's done "right." The kind of mindset doesn't scale, it doesn't inspire, and it sure as hell doesn't build future leaders.

Delegation is not about dumping tasks—it's about developing people.

It's a strategic move, a power shift, and an act of trust. When done right, delegation frees you to focus on what only you can do while empowering others to step into more.

It's not weakness, it's wisdom.

WHY DELEGATION IS A POWER MOVE, NOT A COP-OUT

Let's be clear—letting go isn't easy, especially when you care about excellence. The truth is though, doing everything yourself isn't leadership, it's a bottleneck.

Here's what real delegation does:

It multiplies your impact.

You have twenty-four hours in a day. Delegation allows your vision, standards, and values to ripple through your team, even when you're not in the room. That's influence and that's scale.

It builds trust and ownership.

When you delegate something meaningful, you're saying: *"I trust you with this."* Trust is rocket fuel for confidence. People want to rise when they know you believe in them.

It forces clarity.

You can't delegate well unless you get precise. What needs to be done? By when? What does success look like? Clear delegation strengthens communication and removes the guesswork.

It grows other leaders.

Delegation isn't just about moving tasks—it's about creating momentum for someone else. Every delegated responsibility is a chance for someone to level up.

It frees you to lead forward.

When you're buried in tasks, you can't think strategically. Delegation gives you the space to be creative, visionary, and proactive—the stuff only you can do.

THE REAL BARRIERS TO DELEGATION (AND HOW TO CRUSH THEM)

Let's call out what's really getting in the way.

Perfectionism

"If I don't do it, it won't get done right."

That voice in your head is lying to you. People don't learn by being sidelined. They learn by doing. Yes, there might be mistakes. So, what? That's how you got better, too.

Fear of looking lazy or replaceable

Real talk—smart leaders don't fear being replaced—they build people up so they can rise. When you delegate well, you don't look lazy, you look like a leader who gets it.

Control issues

This one hurts, right? But let it sink in. Control often stems from insecurity. Delegation is the practice of trust. Start small, release a little, and then a little more. Over time, you'll build a machine that doesn't break when you step away.

HOW TO DELEGATE EFFECTIVELY

Delegation is a skill—and like any skill, it can be learned and mastered.

Choose the Right Task

Delegate work that someone else can do 80–90% as well as you—or better. Bonus points if it gives them a stretch opportunity.

Pick the Right Person

Know your people. Delegation is like coaching, it only works when you assign the right mission to the right player.

Be Clear on Expectations

What's the goal? When's it due? How will we measure success? Vague delegation creates frustration and rework. Clarity creates freedom.

Provide the Tools and Authority

If someone's going to run with the ball, don't make them sprint barefoot. Give them the resources, access, and decision-making power they need.

Follow Up, Don't Micromanage

Set milestones or check-ins, but don't hover. Let people breathe. Micromanagement kills morale *and* creativity.

MY DELEGATION SHIFT: FROM ASSISTANT TO DEPUTY COMMISSIONER

I'll never forget the moment Andre Early, our Commissioner, told us he was stepping down to take a new opportunity. We were thrilled for him but the moment he walked out of that office, I felt it—a shift.

We'd gone from three Commissioners to two. Terrance Jackson was promoted from Deputy to Commissioner, and I was elevated from Assistant Commissioner to Deputy.

At first, we figured we'd hire someone to fill my old role. But if you've ever worked in government, you know funding doesn't move at the speed of need. The money never came and the hire didn't happen. Suddenly, we had a hole in leadership with no reinforcements coming.

The default option was obvious, do more ourselves.

But that's not leadership, that's martyrdom.

Terrance and I sat down and made a different decision—we were going to master delegation.

We started by breaking down my old job description, line by line. Some responsibilities went to Terrance while some came to me, but that still left a ton of operational, strategic, and logistical tasks uncovered.

We took a step back and asked: *Who on this team is ready for more?*

Here's the key, we didn't just offload—we elevated.

We chose three team members and designed new roles for each of them based on their strengths. We didn't spring it on them either—we brought them into the conversation, explained the "why" behind the shift, and asked for input. We even held a few brainstorming meetings to reimagine what the department could look like under the new workflow.

That's what real delegation looks like.

It's not just shifting tasks. It's building buy-in and it's creating structure. It's saying: *"I trust you enough to build with you."*

It worked. Each team member owned their new responsibilities and made them better than we could have. They didn't just manage the extra workload, they thrived.

Here's what makes me proud to this day—two out of those three employees were promoted within the next few years.

That's not coincidence, it's the power of delegated opportunity done right.

It didn't just lighten our load, it grew our people.

It built a more agile, resilient, and engaged team.

It made us better leaders.

Looking back, that season taught me more about leadership than any training ever could. Delegation wasn't the soft option. It was the smart one and in this case, it turned out to be the most strategic leadership decision we made that year.

SIMON SINEK'S TAKE ON DELEGATION AND LEADERSHIP

Simon Sinek, renowned leadership expert and author of *Start with Why*, has a quote that's stuck with me for years:

"Leadership is not about being in charge. It is about taking care of those in your charge."

That perspective redefines delegation.

Sinek reminds us that leadership isn't about control or superiority—it's about responsibility to people. Delegation, in that light, is one of the greatest gifts you can offer as a leader. You're saying: *"I see something in you. Let's grow it."*

When you delegate, you're not stepping back—you're lifting up.

FINAL THOUGHT

If leadership is influence—and it is—then delegation is how you spread that influence through others. It's how you multiply impact, cultivate talent, and create space for yourself to think bigger and lead better.

You cannot scale what you refuse to release.

You cannot grow a team by doing everything yourself.

You sure as hell can't evolve if you're chained to every detail.

Let go—not recklessly but intentionally.

That's how you lead forward.

ACTION STEP

Identify one task or area you're holding onto that someone else could take over either to grow their skill set, free up your time, or bring a new perspective. Write it down.

Then do this:

- Pick the right person for it.
- Clearly outline what needs to be done, by when, and what success looks like.
- Explain the 'why' behind the delegation so it's empowering, not dumping.
- Give them space *and* support. Let them run, but don't disappear.
- Follow up after completion to celebrate what went well and reflect on lessons learned.

Journal how it felt to delegate and how the other person responded.

What would you do the same or differently next time?

REFLECTION QUESTION

What's one thing you're currently doing out of habit or control that someone else could take on and how might their growth unlock yours?

FEEDBACK

THE MIRROR EVERY LEADER NEEDS

Leadership isn't about being perfect. It's about being self-aware—and that awareness often comes from feedback.

If you're serious about growth, you can't afford to fear feedback. The best leaders crave it. They know that without it, blind spots stay blind, progress slows, and relationships crack. Feedback is a mirror—it reflects what you might not see on your own. And while it's not always easy to look into, it's one of the most powerful tools for transformation.

WHY FEEDBACK MATTERS IN LEADERSHIP

Sharpen Self-Awareness

Leadership starts with knowing yourself—your strengths, your gaps, and your impact. No matter how self-reflective you are though, you'll never see yourself fully without others. Feedback brings your impact into view.

Build Trust and Connection

Asking for and accepting feedback signals humility. It says, "I don't have all the answers, and I'm open to better ways." That vulnerability builds respect, connection, and trust with your team, peers, and mentors.

Create a Culture of Growth

If you're defensive when you receive feedback, you shut down learning in your organization. If you embrace it and model how to apply it, you normalize growth. Your team starts to see feedback not as criticism but as a catalyst.

Improve Results

You can't fix what you don't know is broken. From performance reviews to casual check-ins, good feedback helps people correct course, optimize execution, and elevate the work. It's the fastest route to continuous improvement.

THE FEEDBACK THAT CHANGED ME

I'm a doer. I move fast, I'm blunt, I speak clearly, and I get things done. In business, in leadership, and in life, I've always operated with intensity. I'm the bull who charges—and for a long time, I believed that was enough.

I knew what I was doing and I had results to show. My team knew the standards I held, and I rarely missed, but there was one part of my leadership I hadn't fully dialed into—my emotional tone.

It was a regular Tuesday. We were onboarding a new employee, and I had a long list of items that needed to be executed to hit our target timeline. I was running from one meeting to the next, checking off tasks, moving quickly, and firing off emails as I went. I sent one to HR about the onboarding deadline. Everything in the message was accurate and I was spot on in what I was conveying. The information was timely, it was correct, and it was precise.

But the tone?

It was cold.

I cc'd the Commissioner to keep everyone informed. That's always been my style—transparent communication, but just three minutes later, he walked into my office and gently closed the door.

"Can we talk?"

My heart rate spiked since you never quite know where these types of conversations are headed.

He sat down calmly and said, "Dave, there's nothing to be nervous about. I just want to support you with something."

Then, he said something that hit me in a way I'll never forget.

He said, "You're not wrong. What you said in that email is all correct but there's no humanity in it. If you want people to work with you and for you, you can't just deliver commands. You have to be human. You have to be kind, be gentle, and ask questions. Don't just force-feed a deadline and sign off with a 'thank you.' You'll be last on someone's list. If you approach people with empathy though, you'll stay a top priority."

That conversation was a gut check.

Not because I was wrong in substance but because I had missed the spirit.

I hadn't realized how robotic I sounded when I was locked into execution mode. I didn't recognize that my tone—even with the right message—could diminish the relationship. I wasn't aware that by neglecting emotional intelligence, I was limiting my leadership potential.

That feedback changed me.

From that day forward, I became intentional with my emails. I started asking, "How do I want this person to feel when they read this?" I paused before I hit send. I re-read messages through the lens of empathy. I started including context, softening the tone, and making sure people didn't just hear what I was saying but could feel the respect behind it.

Feedback doesn't just correct behavior. It develops character.

And I'm grateful someone cared enough to give it.

THE ANATOMY OF GREAT FEEDBACK

Not all feedback is created equal. To grow leaders—not just inform them—you need to deliver and receive feedback with intention.

Make It Timely

Feedback is most effective when it's given close to the moment. Don't let it sit. When correction or praise happens weeks later, the impact fades.

Make It Specific

"Good job" is nice, but it doesn't teach. "The way you handled that conflict with patience and clarity was powerful—that's what I'd love to see more of," is better. Specificity fuels growth.

Make It Safe

Feedback is hard to digest if it feels like an attack. Use "I" language. Focus on behaviors, not identities. Create a culture where feedback is expected, not feared.

Make It Actionable

If people walk away unclear on what to change, they won't change anything. Good feedback ends with clarity, "Here's what worked, here's what didn't, and here's what to do next."

HOW TO RECEIVE FEEDBACK LIKE A LEADER

You're not just a giver of feedback—you have to be a receiver, too. How you receive it determines whether you grow or stay stuck.

Here's how to receive feedback with strength:

Listen Without Defending

You can always evaluate the feedback later—but in the moment, listen with curiosity, not a rebuttal.

Look for the Truth

Even if feedback is messy or emotionally charged, there's often a signal inside the noise.

Say Thank You

It takes courage to give feedback. Honor that courage.

Reflect and Apply

Take time to journal or talk through what you heard. Then put it to use. Don't let insights die in the notebook.

FINAL THOUGHT

Feedback isn't an insult, it's an investment.

It's not a critique of who you are, it's a chance to become who you're meant to be.

If you want to lead well, you have to be willing to look in the mirror and invite others to hold it up for you. You have to love growth more than comfort and you have to be willing to hear the hard things that help you become a softer, stronger, wiser version of yourself.

The greatest leaders aren't the ones who know it all—they're the ones humble enough to keep learning, and strong enough to take the heat.

ACTION STEP

Think back to the last time you received feedback, positive or constructive. How did you respond?

This week, ask someone you trust for direct feedback on your leadership, "What's one thing I'm doing well and one thing I could do better?"

Listen without interrupting and then reflect, apply, and say thank you.

REFLECTION QUESTION

What's one piece of feedback you've received that shaped your leadership and how did it change you?

LEADERSHIP PRESENCE
BE THE CALM IN THE CHAOS

Leadership presence isn't about title, loudness, or bravado. It's about how people feel when you walk into a room and how they remember you when you leave. It's your energy, your clarity, and your conviction. The best leaders don't just talk, they embody confidence, control, and calm in a way that others instinctively trust.

Whether you're leading a team meeting, managing a crisis, or simply showing up for your family, your presence either elevates the room or adds to the noise.

WHY LEADERSHIP PRESENCE MATTERS

It Builds Instant Trust

People instinctively trust leaders who remain composed under pressure. Think about the last time you felt calm around someone when everything else was chaotic. That feeling isn't accidental, it's the power of presence. In moments of uncertainty, your calm presence acts like a lighthouse in a storm, guiding others through turbulence, signaling safety, stability, and reliability.

It Influences Without Force

Effective leadership isn't about yelling louder or flexing authority. It's about subtle signals that say, "I'm steady. I've got this." Great leaders rarely need to raise their voice or exert dominance because their presence speaks volumes through posture, tone, eye contact, and calm confidence. This influence is magnetic because it invites people to follow, not because it demands it.

It Enhances Communication

Your message only lands if your presence supports it. A nervous, scattered, or agitated leader creates noise that drowns out the message. A leader who projects clarity, confidence, and calmness makes others lean in, listen, and remember. Presence gives your words weight.

It's Contagious

Emotions spread like wildfire. Calm leaders foster calm teams and focused leaders build focused cultures. Your emotional energy sets the tone for those around you. If you want to shift a room or a culture, start by shifting your presence.

THE CORE ELEMENTS OF LEADERSHIP PRESENCE

Stillness Under Pressure

When the unexpected hits, do you react impulsively or respond thoughtfully? Presence is your ability to stay grounded when others feel scattered—it's the pause before action, the breath before the response. This stillness isn't passivity, it's powerful control.

Clear, Confident Body Language

Presence is not just what you say, but how you show up. Eye contact that holds attention, posture that communicates strength, movements that are intentional, not fidgety or rushed. Stand tall, speak with intention, and listen fully. Presence is felt before words are even spoken.

Emotional Control

Presence doesn't mean suppressing your feelings. It means owning them without letting them control you, and it means taking a breath when anger or stress rise, rather than letting those emotions hijack your leadership. When you can regulate your emotions, others will instinctively trust your steadiness.

Authenticity

People know when you're "putting on" leadership like a costume. Presence is about being real—flaws, strengths, and all—and leading from that authentic place. Authentic presence connects on a human level and builds lasting loyalty.

Command Without Arrogance

True presence is rooted in humility and clarity, it's not about dominating the room or forcing your will. It's about anchoring the space so others feel safe to be their best selves. A leader with presence holds authority softly yet firmly.

EXPERT INSIGHT AND EXAMPLE

Dr. Amy Cuddy, a social psychologist known for her TED Talk "Your Body Language May Shape Who You Are," explores how our nonverbal behaviors influence both how others perceive us and how we feel inside. Her research on "power posing" shows that by adopting expansive, confident postures—even when you don't initially feel confident—you can boost your brain's feelings of power and reduce stress hormones. This biological shift improves performance and the ability to lead.

Presence also connects deeply to emotional intelligence, a concept popularized by psychologist Daniel Goleman. Emotional intelligence involves self-awareness, self-regulation, empathy, and social skills which are all critical ingredients for presence. Leaders with high emotional intelligence are able to read the room, manage their emotional impact, and connect authentically with others.

Consider Nelson Mandela, a global symbol of leadership presence. After twenty seven years in prison, he emerged without bitterness or anger but with calm dignity, clarity of purpose, and profound humility. His presence transcended words and policies; it inspired a nation to heal. Mandela's presence was the anchor for a deeply fractured country.

MY PERSONAL STORY ON LEADERSHIP PRESENCE – HOW SHOWING UP SHIFTED EVERYTHING

When I first started in government, I was hired as a Recreation Leader—a role where shorts, sweats, and T-shirts were the norm. It was a casual, laid-back environment where few gave much thought to appearances or leadership presence.

I knew I wanted more though. I didn't want to *just* hold a title, I wanted to embody leadership. On day one, I made a conscious choice to show up differently. I wore slacks and a tucked-in button-down shirt. It was a small change with a big message.

At first, people laughed. Some peers made jokes about me being "too formal" or "trying too hard," but I stayed consistent. Day after day, I showed up with the same quiet confidence and intentionality.

I took my administrative role seriously. I didn't just show up and wait for tasks, I *owned* the responsibility. I followed up with program participants to see how they were doing. I proactively asked parents for feedback on youth programs to improve their experience. I spoke clearly and professionally. I looked like a leader and more importantly, I talked like one.

When it was time to run a basketball clinic or coach a game, I switched attire because presence isn't about rigidity but knowing when and how to lead effectively. This flexibility showed my authenticity.

That small, consistent choice sent a loud message not just to others, but to myself. It told me, *I'm ready. I'm serious. I respect this role and my responsibility*. It shifted how others saw me, but more importantly, it shifted how I saw myself.

Within three years, I was promoted twice to a leadership level no one else in the town had reached starting as a recreation leader. Presence was my fast track to success because it's the silent language of leadership. It builds trust before you even have to prove yourself with results.

This story taught me that leadership presence isn't about perfection or authority, it's about showing up consistently, clearly, and with genuine care. It's a leadership superpower accessible to anyone willing to own their space and their responsibility.

FINAL THOUGHT

You don't need to be the loudest voice in the room to lead. You need to be the calm anchor others turn to when everything feels uncertain.

Leadership presence isn't about impressing, it's about anchoring. It's about showing up so powerfully that people feel safe, seen, and led just by being near you.

Presence is a daily practice, a conscious choice, and one of the most powerful leadership tools you have.

ACTION STEP

Before your next important interaction, whether it's a meeting, phone call, or conversation, *pause.* Take sixty seconds, breathe deeply, find stillness, walk in with intention, shoulders back, clear mind, and eyes up. Lead with presence, not pressure.

REFLECTION QUESTION

Think about a time when your presence affected the energy in the room.

What changed in how others responded to you?

What's one specific way you can strengthen your presence tomorrow?

SERVICE-BASED LEADERSHIP
LEAD BY LIFTING OTHERS

Leadership isn't about standing above people, it's about standing *with* them and more importantly, *for* them.

Service-based leadership flips the traditional hierarchy on its head. Instead of leading from a throne, you lead from the trenches. You roll up your sleeves, tune into your people's needs, and act—not for applause, not for recognition, but because it's the right thing to do. It's one of the most humbling yet powerful forms of leadership there is.

This kind of leadership might not be flashy or attention-grabbing. It doesn't rely on titles, loud proclamations, or grand gestures but the results are deep, lasting, and real. Service-based leaders create cultures where trust flourishes, people feel valued, and teams achieve beyond what they thought possible.

WHY SERVICE-BASED LEADERSHIP WORKS

People follow leaders for two fundamental reasons—*trust* and *belief*.

Trust grows when others feel you genuinely prioritize them.

Belief is earned when they see you act consistently on their behalf.

This leadership style is not soft. It requires strength, courage, and humility. Service-based leadership demands that you set your ego aside, you take on uncomfortable, sometimes thankless roles, and you pour into others even when your own cup feels empty.

Here's the truth—when you serve, you *scale*. You scale influence, culture, and impact—not by shouting louder, but by lifting others higher.

THE DIFFERENCE BETWEEN BOSSES AND LEADERS

It's easy to confuse leadership with authority, but there's a stark difference:

A **boss** gives orders; a **leader** asks questions.

A **boss** looks for fault; a **leader** takes responsibility.

A **boss** demands loyalty; a **leader** earns it through service, consistency, and genuine care.

Rooted in service, leadership becomes relational—not positional. It's not just about what you say—it's about *how* you show up every day.

THE STORY THAT CHANGED HOW I SEE SERVICE

I want to share a story I witnessed years ago—one that shaped my understanding of what real leadership looks like.

I was in college, riding in a car with my roommates on a cold winter day. We had the heater on, bundled up, the windows mostly up, and we were jamming out to our favorite music, laughing, and having fun. As we waited at a stoplight, I saw a mother and her young child trying to cross an icy street nearby.

The mom was limping, weighed down by bags. The little boy was barely tall enough to hold her hand and was carefully navigating the slippery ice. Watching them struggle, I knew everyone around saw what was happening and likely had the same thought—to help. Unfortunately, it's just one of those things people don't always do.

Although I didn't step out to assist—caught up in my youthful distractions—someone else quietly did. A man, without fanfare or expectation, approached them calmly. He helped steady the mother, took some bags from her arms, and even gave the child the jacket off his own back to keep him warm. He didn't announce it or seek thanks. He simply *served*.

That moment hit me hard—not because I did something, but because I *didn't*. I was too immature then to recognize the leadership opportunity right in front of me. I missed the chance to lead by serving, to make a meaningful difference. The other man's quiet action showed me leadership happens everywhere, it's not reserved for titles or offices. Leadership is a choice and a responsibility we all carry.

I promised myself at that moment, the next time a similar opportunity came, I wouldn't miss it.

TIM DUNCAN: THE GOLD STANDARD IN SERVICE-BASED LEADERSHIP

This quiet, consistent form of leadership reminds me of Tim Duncan, one of the greatest basketball players and leaders of all time.

Duncan's nickname was "The Big Fundamental," and not because he was flashy or attention-seeking. He was the steady hand on the Spurs' dynasty, the player who led not through loud speeches but through actions. He was known for doing the hard, often unseen work— setting screens, playing tough defense, and lifting up teammates without stealing the spotlight.

Tim Duncan embodied service-based leadership. His humility, work ethic, and selflessness set the tone for the entire team. His teammates trusted him implicitly because he *showed up* every day for them, in every practice, in every game. He led not by commanding but by serving and making those around him better.

The results? Five NBA championships and a culture of excellence that lasted decades. His leadership didn't just win games, it built a legacy, and that's the power of service-based leadership. It creates impact that outlasts any one person.

THE 5 CORE PRINCIPLES OF SERVICE-BASED LEADERSHIP

If you want to lead by serving, these five principles will guide your way:

Lead From the Front

Don't ask for commitment you aren't willing to give. Your people are watching more than they're listening. Be the example in both word and action.

Ask, Don't Assume

Curiosity is a superpower. Ask your team or those you lead, *"What's standing in your way?"* *"How can I support you?"* Often, the needs are simpler than you think.

Create a Safe Environment

People perform best when they feel safe to speak up, make mistakes, and grow. Create space for honest feedback, authenticity, and experimentation—without fear or pretense.

Act Without Expectation

Serve because it's who you are, not because you want recognition. Real leaders don't keep score—they lead generously, knowing the payoff comes in trust, culture, and character.

Serve the Mission First

Service isn't about people-pleasing, it's about aligning every action with the mission, even when it's hard or unpopular. That clarity anchors your leadership.

HOW SERVICE-BASED LEADERSHIP TRANSLATES TO RESULTS

Leaders who serve see their teams move faster, stronger, and with more unity. When people know you've got their back, they take bigger risks, collaborate more openly, and show up fully.

Tim Duncan's Spurs weren't just a collection of talent—they were a family that trusted their leader implicitly. That trust, born of Duncan's servant leadership, translated into resilience in tough games, seamless teamwork, and championships.

Similarly, when you lead by lifting others—whether at work, in your family, or your community—you unlock potential that no amount of top-down command can match.

HOW TO PUT THIS INTO PRACTICE TODAY

You don't need a massive platform or a title to lead through service. Start with *intention*.

Send one message: *"How can I help you win this week?"*

Give one honest, meaningful piece of praise—no fluff, just real acknowledgment.

Remove one obstacle for someone, even if it means extra effort on your part.

Remember—leadership isn't always about making your life easier— it's about making their load lighter so the whole team moves faster.

FINAL THOUGHT

Service doesn't weaken leadership, it *anchors* it. You don't become less powerful when you serve, you become more magnetic, more trusted, and more influential.

You lead best when your people know you're willing to go to war with them, not just watch from the sidelines.

ACTION STEP

Ask one person today:

"What's something you're struggling with right now that I can help you move forward?"

Then listen, act, and follow up. Show them what service looks like in real time.

REFLECTION QUESTION

Think about a time you witnessed service-based leadership—whether by a stranger, a colleague, or a friend.

How did their actions impact you or those around them?

How can you embody that same spirit in your leadership journey today?

EMOTIONAL INTELLIGENCE
MASTER YOURSELF, LEAD OTHERS

The best leaders aren't the loudest in the room.

They're the most emotionally steady—the ones who don't crumble under pressure, lash out in conflict, or spiral when things go sideways. They know when to speak, when to stay silent, when to push, and when to let things breathe.

That kind of leadership doesn't come from titles or tenure, it comes from emotional intelligence—the ability to understand and manage your own emotions, while recognizing and responding to the emotions of others.

This skill is often underestimated, but when it comes to actual leadership performance, it's a game-changer.

As Katherine Cepeda, author of *Elevated Glow: Transform from the Inside Out*, puts it:

"When emotions are high, intelligence is low."

That one sentence explains why so many leaders fail when the heat rises. You might be brilliant with the perfect strategy, but if you lose your cool, your influence shrinks, your team pulls back, and the moment is lost.

WHY EMOTIONAL INTELLIGENCE IS A LEADERSHIP SUPERPOWER

Studies back it up. According to research from TalentSmart, emotional intelligence accounts for 58% of performance in all types of jobs. In fact, 90% of top performers have high EQ (Emotional Quotient), not just high IQ (Intelligence Quotient). EQ measures how well you connect with people, handle stress, and navigate the emotional side of leadership and life while IQ measures cognitive intelligence. EQ isn't just a soft skill—it's strategic impact.

Leaders with high EQ:

- Keep their cool under pressure
- Defuse tension without folding
- Make people feel seen, heard, and valued
- Navigate hard conversations without destroying relationships
- Make better decisions because they're not clouded by emotional noise

When you master EQ, you lead with presence. You become the calm in the chaos and the anchor in the storm.

THE 4 CORE PILLARS OF EQ

Self-Awareness

The ability to recognize your own emotions in the moment, and understand how they impact your thoughts and behavior.

Ask yourself: *"What am I really feeling right now—and why?"*

Self-Regulation

The ability to manage those emotions, especially when triggered. Not bottling emotions but channeling them productively.

Ask: *"Is this response helpful—or just a release?"*

Social Awareness

The ability to read the room—to understand unspoken needs, group dynamics, and the emotional undercurrents beneath words.

Ask: *"What's not being said right now that I need to hear?"*

Relationship Management

The ability to communicate clearly, build trust, handle conflict, and influence others from a place of respect.

Ask: *"How do I make this person feel safe enough to be honest—and motivated enough to act?"*

REAL-WORLD EQ: A PERSONAL STORY

I thought I had it all under control but I didn't.

One night, not too long ago, I got loud—too loud—with the one person who looks up to me the most. *My daughter.*

We were at home, she was playing, being her vibrant, curious, wild self, but I was drained and I was frustrated. There were a hundred things swirling in my head from deadlines and responsibilities to unspoken stress.

Something insignificant happened. Maybe it was because she spilled something or maybe she said "no" one too many times but I snapped—my voice rose, my energy shifted. I didn't yell at her, I *exploded* on her.

She froze.

Her little shoulders tensed up, her eyes welled with tears, and she started shaking.

In that moment, my heart shattered.

I had become the storm—not the shelter, not the calm, and not the dad I swore I'd be.

She wasn't being difficult, she was being a kid. I was the one who failed to manage my emotions. I let stress override presence, I let pressure dictate behavior, and I let ego lead instead of love.

That night, I held her and apologized. I told her I was wrong. I told her that even dads mess up and when we do, we own it. I cried when she fell asleep and when I looked in the mirror, I didn't see a leader, I saw someone who still had work to do.

That moment changed me.

Not because of guilt but because of clarity. I realized that emotional intelligence isn't just for the office or the stage it's for the dinner table, the bedtime routine, and the car ride home. It's for every moment that matters and every relationship that counts.

LEADERSHIP IN ACTION: THE DEMAR DEROZAN EXAMPLE

In the world of professional sports, emotional intensity is a given. But leadership? That's where EQ shows up. One powerful example is NBA All-Star DeMar DeRozan.

DeRozan made headlines not just for his performance on the court, but for his willingness to speak openly about his mental health struggles, including depression and anxiety. He didn't hide his emotions, he used them to connect. In doing so, he became a powerful emotional leader for his teammates.

When his former teammate Kyle Lowry was struggling, DeRozan didn't give a motivational speech, he just listened. No judgment, just presence. That trust helped build one of the strongest bonds in the league.

Emotional intelligence isn't just about managing your own storms, it's about helping others weather theirs. DeRozan models that truth with every quiet moment of care, every honest interview, and every relationship he nurtures behind the scenes.

HOW TO BUILD EQ DAILY

Name It to Tame It

The moment you can name your emotion—anger, fear, guilt, impatience—you begin to disarm it. Language turns chaos into clarity.

The 10-Second Rule

When triggered, count to ten. Breathe and then ask: "What outcome do I want here?" Act from purpose, not impulse.

Empathic Listening

Let people finish their thoughts, reflect back what you heard, and show them they matter—not because you agree, but because you're present.

Track Emotional Patterns

Journal your emotional highs and lows, identify the triggers, and recognize the patterns. This turns experience into self-mastery.

Give Grace Without Lowering Standards

EQ doesn't mean avoiding hard truths, it means delivering them with respect. It means holding people to the standard, without making them feel like a failure.

FINAL THOUGHT

Emotional intelligence isn't soft, it's strong.

It's not about being passive, it's about being precise.

It's not about avoiding hard conversations, it's about navigating them with wisdom, composure, and care.

Leadership starts with mastering the hardest person to lead—*yourself.*

When you can regulate your own state, you liberate others, and you become safe, steady, and strong.

You become the leader your people lean on because they know, no matter what, you'll never lose yourself in the heat.

ACTION STEP

Think of a recent moment where your emotions hijacked your leadership. Write down:

- What happened?
- What emotion showed up?
- What did you do—and what could you have done better?

Then choose one person today to be fully present with. No phone, no advice—just *listen.*

REFLECTION QUESTION

When the pressure rises do you lead from reaction, or from response?

What would change if you paused just five more seconds before you spoke?

CONFLICT RESOLUTION
LEAD THROUGH THE FIRE, NOT AROUND IT

Avoiding conflict doesn't make you peaceful, it makes you passive.

Passivity is the enemy of progress.

True leaders don't run from friction, they walk into it with clarity, control, and courage.

Conflict is often misunderstood in leadership. It's seen as a problem to be avoided rather than an opportunity to be harnessed. Conflict though, when managed intentionally, is one of the greatest tools for clarity, growth, and innovation.

WHY CONFLICT IS INEVITABLE—AND NECESSARY

Whenever people care, conflict will surface. It is the natural byproduct of differing ideas, values, priorities, and personalities working together. Rather than fearing it, leaders need to embrace conflict as a sign of engagement and passion.

Research from CPP Global—the makers of the Thomas-Kilmann Conflict Mode Instrument—reveals that 85% of employees experience conflict at work. Even more striking is

the financial toll— unresolved conflict drains organizations in
the U.S. alone of up to $359 billion annually in lost
productivity.

This statistic isn't just a number, it's a wake-up call. Leaders who
ignore or mishandle conflict are bleeding their teams dry, often
without realizing it.

An absence of conflict may seem ideal, but it's usually a red flag
signaling that people are either emotionally checked out and disen-
gaged, or they're afraid to speak honestly, suppressing concerns to
"keep the peace."

Neither scenario fosters a healthy, high-performing culture. The
absence of conflict is often a symptom of a deeper problem—lack of
psychological safety.

THE REAL COST OF AVOIDING CONFLICT

Avoiding conflict can feel easier in the moment but long-term, it's a
toxic strategy.

Unchecked conflict:

- Saps morale as frustrations simmer beneath the surface
- Breaks down communication as people withdraw
- Breeds resentment that damages relationships and trust
- Kills productivity as collaboration stalls

Research by CPP also shows that employees spend an average of 2.8
hours per week managing conflict. That's over $300 billion in lost
wages yearly just in the U.S.—wages spent not creating, innovating,
or delivering value, but dealing with avoidable conflict.

The cost is not just financial, it's emotional. A culture that fears
conflict breeds silence, apathy, and stagnation.

THE CONFLICT RESOLUTION FORMULA: C.A.L.M.

Conflict doesn't have to be a war zone. It can be a gateway to deeper understanding and stronger bonds.

Here's the C.A.L.M. formula to lead through conflict effectively:

C – Clarify the Issue

Avoid emotional spirals. Get specific. What *actually* happened? What's the root cause beneath the surface reaction? Ask questions to gather facts, not assumptions.

A – Address the Person, Not Their Identity

Attack the behavior, not the person.

Say: "When this happened, it caused this impact..."

Don't say: "You're careless." This prevents defensiveness and keeps focus on solutions.

L – Listen Without Reloading

Don't spend your time crafting a rebuttal. Listen deeply and reflect their words back to confirm understanding. Most tension dissolves when people feel heard.

M – Move Toward Resolution

Ask: "What do you need to move forward?" and "Here's what I need."

Set clear next steps. Hold standards firmly but let go of grudges.

HOW HIGH-LEVEL LEADERS EMBRACE CONFLICT

Top leaders see conflict as data, not drama.

Here's what they do:

- Address issues early, before resentment takes hold
- Stay calm under pressure and hold emotional intelligence front and center
- Separate the problem from the person, keeping relationships intact
- Seek to strengthen relationships, not win fights

Harvard professor Amy Edmondson, a leading expert on psychological safety, highlights that teams who openly discuss conflicts without fear outperform others significantly. When team members feel safe to speak up, innovation and trust soar.

REAL-WORLD EXAMPLE: THE MISSED DEADLINES

Consider a colleague repeatedly missing deadlines, impacting the whole team.

Instead of gossiping or snapping, you say:

"I've noticed the last two deadlines were missed. It's putting the project behind and creating extra pressure. Can we talk about what's going on and how we can fix it?"

This invites honesty and collaboration instead of blame and it models calm, clear leadership.

PERSONAL STORY: CONFLICT IN A HOSPITAL GOWN

March 3, 2025

I walked into that colonoscopy room expecting peace of mind.

I had cleaned up my life. No alcohol since January 1, 2024 and I was eating clean, training hard, and managing my Crohn's with precision. In my mind, the colonoscopy was just a formality but life has a way of humbling us when we least expect it.

The doctor came back into the room with a paper in his hand and a look on his face I'll never forget. His energy shifted. He wasn't just reviewing results, he was preparing to deliver a blow.

"David," he said. "Although nothing is confirmed yet there *is* cause for concern."

The paper read:

- **High risk for colon cancer**
- **Six polyps**—all over 4mm
- **A white lesion** resembling colon cancer

And then he said the words that hit harder than anything on that page, "We'll follow up in a week with the results."

A *week.*

Seven days to wrestle with uncertainty.

Seven days of wondering if I'd be around to raise my daughter.

Seven days to face a version of myself I hadn't met yet.

Here's what most people miss about leadership—conflict doesn't always show up in a boardroom. Sometimes it shows up in your own body, in your own mind, and at the worst possible time.

I could've shut down and many people would have.

But I took a breath and I leaned in.

I didn't try to control what I couldn't.

I focused on what I *could.* I prayed, I trained, I ate clean, and I talked to the people closest to me. I didn't pretend I was okay, I chose to *lead* through it anyway.

When the call finally came five days later, the words felt like divine thunder, "David, you're cancer free. Not only that—your Crohn's is in deep remission."

What the doctor thought looked like cancer was something else entirely. Not only was I okay, I was better than I imagined.

That moment didn't just give me relief, it gave me revelation.

Real leadership isn't about avoiding conflict—it's about embracing it with courage, clarity, and faith.

Whether it's an argument, a diagnosis, a personal storm, or a professional breakdown, conflict will come. What defines you is whether you *run from it or walk through it with your head high and your values intact.*

So now, when conflict shows up in my life, I don't flinch.

I remember the paper.

I remember the breath.

I remember that peace isn't the absence of conflict—it's the presence of purpose inside of it.

CONFLICT AND CULTURE: THE BIGGER PICTURE

The way leaders handle conflict defines their culture.

Are conflicts addressed openly, respectfully, and with curiosity? Or are they ignored, swept under the rug, and met with defensiveness?

Culture expert Edgar Schein emphasizes that true culture change happens when leaders model vulnerability and willingness to engage in difficult conversations.

A culture where conflict is seen as opportunity creates engagement, accountability, and growth. One where it's feared breeds disengagement, blame, and stagnation.

FINAL THOUGHT

Conflict doesn't break teams, it reveals them.

Weak leaders avoid hard conversations.

Great leaders step into them early, often, and well.

Unity isn't built on silence. It's built on navigating discomfort together.

When the heat is on, leadership shows up—choose to lead through the fire, not around it.

ACTION STEP

Identify one unresolved tension—work or personal.

Write down the specific issue.

Note the impact it has on you and others.

Schedule a ten-minute conversation this week using the C.A.L.M. framework.

Go in with no expectation of agreement—only the goal of mutual understanding.

REFLECTION QUESTION

When conflict arises, do you retreat, resist, or respond?

What's one tangible step you can take today to lead through the fire, not around it?

INFLUENCE
LEAD WITHOUT A TITLE

Influence is one of the most misunderstood and underestimated qualities in leadership. It is often confused with authority, power, or rank but the truth is that these are very different things.

Authority is granted while influence is earned.

Anyone can be handed a title, given a corner office, or appointed a team to manage but those things alone do not guarantee respect, trust, or followership. Influence is an invisible currency that can't be bought or bestowed—it's cultivated through character, connection, and consistent action over time.

WHY INFLUENCE MATTERS MORE THAN AUTHORITY

In today's rapidly evolving workplaces and communities, traditional hierarchies are flattening. Teams are more diverse, workplaces more collaborative, and leadership more distributed. Influence, not formal authority, is now the real engine that drives progress.

Consider this—a 2020 study published in the *Journal of Leadership & Organizational Studies* surveyed over twelve hundred employees and found that 70% of workplace influence comes from informal leaders, not those with official titles. These informal leaders guide culture, set the tone for behavior, and inspire discretionary effort from others simply through their presence and consistency.

When you lead with influence, you become the person others turn to —not because they have to, but because they want to. Influence shapes environments, builds trust, and accelerates impact far beyond what positional power can achieve.

THE THREE PILLARS OF INFLUENCE: CHARACTER, CONNECTION, CONSISTENCY

1. Character: The Foundation of Credibility

Dr. Ronald Riggio, a renowned leadership scholar, asserts that "Character is the foundation of true leadership influence." People are drawn to leaders whose words align with their actions and whose integrity is visible and unshakable. When you say you value discipline or kindness, do you demonstrate it daily? Character is the magnet that pulls others in, creating trust and respect.

2. Connection: The Human Bridge

Research from Harvard Business Review shows leaders who genuinely connect with their teams boost engagement by over 20%. Influence blooms in relationships where people feel truly seen and heard. Dr. Susan David, a Harvard psychologist, explains, "Influence is not just about persuasion, it's about empathy and understanding." When you listen deeply and care authentically, you build bridges that enable influence to flow naturally.

3. Consistency: The Power of Reliability

Robert Cialdini, the author of *Influence: The Psychology of Persuasion*, identifies consistency as a critical factor in persuading and influencing others. People crave predictability and reliability—they trust leaders who show up the same way, day after day, especially when it's inconvenient or difficult. Influence is earned in the quiet moments of everyday integrity.

THE STORY OF MS. BEVERLY MCCOY: THE POWER OF EVERYDAY INFLUENCE

If influence is a skill anyone can master, then Ms. Beverly McCoy was a living example of what that looks like in action.

Ms. Bev served as our receptionist for over twenty years and was the very first person anyone saw when they entered our facility. She wasn't simply the gatekeeper of phones and appointments, she was the heart and soul of our culture.

Every day, Ms. Bev greeted people by name, with a genuine smile and kindness that never faltered, no matter what challenges she faced behind the scenes. She set a tone of warmth and professionalism that shaped how employees and visitors felt before they even reached a conference room or office.

Her influence was so profound that when she retired, we began referring to our daily customer service reminders as the "Beverly McCoy Customer Service Reminder." That's how deeply her commitment to excellence and her steady kindness impacted us.

Ms. Bev taught us that influence is less about bold moves and more about consistent small acts of care. She showed up every day—smiling, present, patient—and in doing so, she influenced everyone around her to raise their own standards.

She never sought the spotlight, yet she was the shining star of our workplace culture. It didn't matter what line of work you were in, her influence made a difference because at its core, influence is about presence, empathy, and the daily choices we make to impact those around us positively.

WHAT MS. BEV'S STORY TEACHES US ABOUT INFLUENCE

No matter your role or title, you have influence.

Your impact isn't measured by your rank or position but by how you treat others, the standards you hold yourself to, and your daily commitment to showing up authentically.

Influence ripples outward—from a receptionist who greets warmly, to a teammate who listens deeply, to a leader who models resilience. You can be the Ms. Bev in your workplace, family, or community.

Imagine the collective power if everyone committed to that kind of influence, the kind that transforms environments one interaction at a time.

PRACTICAL TAKEAWAYS FOR BUILDING YOUR INFLUENCE

Make Small Actions Matter

You don't have to make grand gestures to influence. Like Ms. Bev, it's the small daily choices, the smile, the remembered name, and the genuine greeting that build deep trust over time. Don't underestimate the power of these moments.

Be Present Before You Are Heard

Influence begins when you are fully present with people. Stop multi-tasking when someone talks to you. Look them in the eye and listen to understand, not just to respond.

Lead with Empathy

Put yourself in others' shoes regularly. Ask yourself what matters to them and what challenges they face. When people feel understood, your influence multiplies.

Be Relentlessly Consistent

Your influence will grow only if people see you live your values day in and day out. It's easy to be kind or disciplined once. The real power is in the relentless repetition, especially when it's inconvenient.

Communicate Clearly and Honestly

People follow leaders who don't confuse or complicate. Clarity, honesty, and focus create safety and trust, two essential ingredients for influence.

Take Responsibility for Your Impact

Recognize that your mood, attitude, and actions impact the people around you more than you realize. Own that power and choose to use it wisely.

FINAL THOUGHT

Influence isn't flashy or loud. It's the quiet force built by integrity, empathy, and consistency.

You don't need a title to lead. You don't need a position to inspire.

You just need to show up.

Be the influence someone else needs.

ACTION STEP

Identify one person you want to positively influence. Ask yourself:

Do they *trust* me?

Do they know *what I stand for?*

Do I *model* the behavior I expect?

Take one concrete step today—whether it's a thoughtful conversation, a sincere greeting, or delivering on a promise.

REFLECTION QUESTION

What's one small but consistent action can I take today that will deepen my influence in my work, family, or community?

How will I hold myself accountable to showing up with integrity and empathy every day?

INTEGRITY

THE FOUNDATION OF LEADERSHIP

Integrity is the silent force that underpins all great leadership. It is the invisible thread weaving together trust, respect, and loyalty—essential elements that form the backbone of any successful leader.

Integrity is doing the right thing when no one is watching.

It's what defines your character in moments of solitude, during challenges, and when you're faced with difficult choices.

WHAT IS INTEGRITY, REALLY?

Integrity isn't a one-off act or a momentary decision. It's a consistent way of being, a commitment to living by a core set of principles no matter the situation, audience, or convenience.

Dr. Stephen Covey, author of *The 7 Habits of Highly Effective People*, describes integrity as "the value of being honest and having strong moral principles, and the quality of being whole and undivided." He points out that integrity is about "wholeness"—your words, actions, thoughts, and feelings all aligning.

Integrity means personal responsibility, accountability, and courage. It means standing firm on your values even when the easy way is to look the other way. It's shown in small, daily choices—the promises you keep, the honesty you show, the courage to be vulnerable and admit when you're wrong.

This quiet force quietly builds a foundation that holds steady when life and leadership get stormy.

WHY INTEGRITY MATTERS IN LEADERSHIP

Leadership without integrity isn't leadership at all. People don't just want a leader, they want a leader they *can trust.*

Trust is the currency of influence and leadership. When your words and actions align, you build that currency. When they don't, you spend it—sometimes irreparably.

According to a 2023 study by the Edelman Trust Barometer, 79% of employees say that integrity is a critical factor in their trust in leadership. When leaders lose trust, teams falter, communication breaks down, and morale tanks.

Stephen M.R. Covey, who deeply explored trust in his book *The Speed of Trust*, makes a clear case—trust is built on character and competence, and character's foundation is integrity.

Once integrity is compromised, the damage is swift and far-reaching. The ripple effects touch your team, peers, family—even your own self-respect.

Integrity is not just honesty, it's the active, ongoing alignment of your values, words, and actions. It's what separates a leader from a boss, a role model from a title-holder.

INTEGRITY AS A LEADERSHIP TOOL

Trust

Without it, leadership is powerless. Integrity is the foundation of trust. Your team needs to know that your commitments are real and your intentions pure.

Respect

Integrity earns respect. It signals to others that you operate with honor, fairness, and an unwavering commitment to what's right—even when it's costly.

Clarity

When your decisions flow from clear, consistent principles, you lead with confidence and inspire clarity in others.

Consistency

Integrity creates reliability. Your promises aren't just words, they become bonds. This consistency creates a culture where others step up and hold themselves accountable.

HOW INTEGRITY IMPACTS YOUR RELATIONSHIPS

Integrity strengthens relationships across every part of your life. When people see that you walk your talk, they feel safe to follow, to lean in, and to trust.

It's not just a professional tool, it's a personal compass.

How you treat your spouse, friends, colleagues, and even yourself in moments when no one's watching reveals your true character.

Do your actions reflect the values you claim? Are you honest with yourself about where you fall short?

Integrity builds deep, lasting connections based on respect and authenticity.

A PERSONAL STORY: INTEGRITY IN THE HEART OF NYC

In 2024, I was in New York City for an important podcast interview with Michelle Barone on iHeartRadio—a big moment that I'd been working toward for months.

The city was buzzing with its usual chaos, and the challenge of finding parking was intense. I pulled into two lots, both full. I was rushing—time was tight, energy high—and frustration crept in.

Finally, I found a third lot where an older valet attendant, noticing my urgency, made space for my car. He didn't have to but he chose kindness in the middle of a hectic day.

After the interview, I returned to my car with deep gratitude. Normally, I'd tip valets between $3 and $10. But this man had done more than his job; he'd shown me grace in a place where stress and hustle reign.

I pulled a $20 bill from my pocket and handed it to him with heartfelt thanks, "Here you go, man. Thank you, God bless."

His face lit up—it was clearly the best tip he'd received that day.

Then, something unexpected happened.

He looked me straight in the eye and said, "Sir, there was another $20 under that one. Here's your money back."

I was stunned. The integrity in that moment was palpable. Here was a man refusing to accept money that wasn't rightfully his.

I offered the extra $20 again, wanting to honor his kindness but he smiled and said, "Absolutely not. You weren't even here for two hours. Have a great day."

That moment has stayed with me ever since.

It was a reminder that integrity isn't about grand gestures or titles. It's about honoring yourself and others in every moment, even the small, unseen ones.

Too often, we get blinded by noise and distractions, chasing shortcuts and quick wins.

But true integrity *done right* builds the kind of foundation that lasts through any storm.

EXPANDING THE LESSON: WHY INTEGRITY IS HARD—AND WHY IT'S WORTH IT

Integrity demands courage. It's easy to talk about values and principles when things are going well but real integrity shows up in the tough moments:

- When no one's watching, and you have the choice to cut corners
- When you must own a mistake that could cost you
- When the pressure to conform threatens to bend your truth

That's when integrity becomes a muscle you must strengthen, and just like any muscle, it's uncomfortable at first.

Leadership expert Jim Collins, author of *Good to Great*, highlights the importance of what he calls "Level 5 Leadership"—a blend of humility and fierce resolve. Leaders with integrity don't seek the spotlight or easy applause; they do what's right, consistently and humbly, for the long haul.

Integrity is a daily practice—a commitment to choosing what's right over what's convenient, to putting values over ego, and to standing firm even when it costs you.

The payoff?

You become a leader people trust with their time, talents, and hearts.

You build a legacy that outlasts your title or paycheck.

You find peace in knowing you lead not just with your voice, but with your soul.

PRACTICAL TAKEAWAYS: HOW TO BUILD INTEGRITY IN YOUR LEADERSHIP

Reflect Daily

Ask yourself each evening if your actions aligned with your values. Be brutally honest because growth requires clarity.

Own Your Mistakes

Don't hide errors or blame others. Integrity grows when you take responsibility.

Speak Truth with Kindness

Be honest but compassionate. Integrity thrives on truth, not harshness.

Set Boundaries

Say no to what conflicts with your values, even when it's tough.

Be Reliable

Follow through on every promise, no matter how small. Consistency is king.

Lead by Example

Show others what integrity looks like in action. Your culture reflects your example.

FINAL THOUGHT

Integrity is not optional, it's the foundation of who you are as a leader and human being.

Without it, everything else you build is unstable, no matter how impressive it looks on the surface.

Leadership without integrity is a house on sand—doomed to crumble when tested.

But build on integrity—the unshakable rock—and you create a legacy of trust, respect, and impact that endures beyond any challenge.

ACTION STEP

Take a moment today to assess your integrity in one key area of your life—work, family, or personal habits. Ask yourself:

Do my actions reflect my core values?

Am I cutting corners or compromising my standards anywhere?

Are my words and actions consistent, even when no one is watching?

Choose one clear action to reinforce your integrity—follow through on a promise, have an honest conversation, or correct a situation where your actions haven't aligned.

REFLECTION QUESTION

Where in my life am I called to deepen my integrity right now?

What steps will I take to hold myself accountable to living my values fully and consistently?

LEGACY AND IMPACT
CREATING A LIFE THAT MATTERS

"I don't really care if people forget me. My legacy wasn't about me. It was about everything I could do for another."

— Shannon L. Alder

In the whirlwind of daily responsibilities and the relentless pursuit of success, it's easy to become consumed by immediate goals—closing the next deal, launching the next product, achieving the next milestone. Yet, amidst this hustle, a profound question often lingers in the background, *"What will I leave behind?"*

Leadership transcends personal achievements and accolades. It's about the imprint we leave on others—the values we instill, the inspiration we provide, and the lives we touch. Legacy isn't a distant concept reserved for the end of one's career or life; it's something we craft daily through our actions, decisions, and interactions.

UNDERSTANDING LEGACY

Legacy is the culmination of our life's work, values, and the impact we've had on others. It's not measured by the wealth we've accumulated or the titles we've held, but by the positive changes we've inspired and the people we've uplifted.

Consider this—every interaction you have, every decision you make, contributes to your legacy. It's the mentor who guided a young professional, the leader who stood by their team during challenging times, the individual who chose integrity over convenience. These moments, though seemingly small, weave together to form a tapestry of lasting impact.

THE LEGACY OF APPLE AND STEVE JOBS

To illustrate the power of legacy, let's reflect on the story of Apple Inc. and its visionary co-founder, Steve Jobs. Apple's journey offers a compelling narrative of how values and vision can shape not just a company, but the world.

When Jobs returned to Apple in 1997, the company was on the brink of collapse. Through his relentless pursuit of innovation and excellence, he transformed Apple into one of the most influential companies globally. But beyond the groundbreaking products—the iMac, iPod, iPhone, and iPad—Jobs instilled a culture that prioritized simplicity, user experience, and design elegance.

Jobs believed that technology should be intuitive and accessible. He once said, "Simple can be harder than complex: You have to work hard to get your thinking clean to make it simple." This philosophy permeated Apple's products, making them not just tools, but extensions of human creativity and expression.

Even after his passing in 2011, Jobs' legacy continues to influence Apple's direction. The company's commitment to innovation, design, and user-centric products remains unwavering. This enduring impact underscores that true legacy isn't confined to one's lifetime; it lives on through the values and culture one establishes.

A PERSONAL LEGACY: LESSONS FROM MY GRANDFATHER

While corporate legacies like Apple's are monumental, personal legacies are equally profound. I'd like to share the story of my grandfather, a Navy veteran and police sergeant, whose influence shaped my understanding of leadership and integrity.

During my seventh and eighth-grade years, my grandfather often drove me to school. Those morning rides were more than just commutes, they were lessons in character and values. Two principles he consistently emphasized were:

Be strong in everything you do.

Love your family.

He taught me that strength wasn't about dominance or aggression, but about standing firm in one's beliefs, protecting those who are vulnerable, and facing challenges with courage. Simultaneously, he emphasized the importance of love—being present for family, showing compassion, and nurturing relationships.

My grandfather embodied the balance between a lion and a lamb. To outsiders, he might have seemed formidable, but to those who knew him, he was a source of unwavering support and warmth. His leadership wasn't about authority; it was about service, commitment, and love.

When he passed away, our family felt an immense void. Yet, his teachings and values continue to guide us. His legacy isn't just remembered, it's lived.

WHY LEGACY MATTERS IN LEADERSHIP

As leaders, our influence extends beyond immediate results. The culture we cultivate, the values we uphold, and the people we mentor all contribute to our legacy.

Inspiring Future Generations

Just as my grandfather's teachings continue to guide me, the values we instill in others can influence generations to come.

Creating Lasting Change

Leaders who prioritize impact over personal gain drive transformations that outlive their tenure.

Building Meaningful Connections

Genuine relationships, built on trust and empathy, form the foundation of a lasting legacy.

Empowering Others

By mentoring and uplifting others, we ensure that our influence multiplies, fostering a culture of continuous growth and leadership.

BUILDING YOUR LEGACY

Crafting a meaningful legacy requires intentionality:

Live by Your Values

Consistency between words and actions builds trust and respect.

Mentor and Teach

Share your knowledge and experiences to guide others on their journeys.

Make a Difference

Engage in initiatives that align with your values and contribute positively to your community.

Reflect Regularly

Periodically assess your actions and decisions to ensure they align with the legacy you wish to leave.

FINAL THOUGHT

Legacy isn't about being remembered; it's about making a difference. It's the culmination of our choices, actions, and the lives we've touched. Whether through leading a global company like Apple or sharing wisdom during morning drives, our legacy is built daily.

ACTION STEP

Take a moment today to reflect:

What values define you?

How do your daily actions align with these values?

Who have you mentored or positively influenced recently?

Now, choose one action that reinforces your desired legacy. It could be reaching out to a mentee, initiating a community project, or simply expressing gratitude to someone who has impacted you.

REFLECTION QUESTION

If your leadership journey ended today, what stories would others share about you?

Are those the stories you want to be told?

LESSON 30
ACTION
THE KEY TO EVERYTHING

Talk is cheap, plans are comforting, but nothing—absolutely nothing—changes until you take action.

Action is the great separator. It's the bridge between who you are and who you're capable of becoming. It's where goals become growth, and where intention turns into transformation. Leadership, success, healing, rebuilding—all of it is built on the unshakeable foundation of action.

WHY ACTION IS THE ULTIMATE DIFFERENCE MAKER

You've probably heard this before, "Ideas are worthless without execution." It's more than just a catchy quote, it's a brutal truth. The world is full of dreamers. People with notebooks full of plans, people who talk big about what they're going to do "one day," people who wait for motivation or the perfect time.

But the ones who actually change things? They do. They act, they fail, they get back up, and they take imperfect steps forward, every day.

Leadership, growth, and personal excellence don't belong to the smartest people or the most privileged. They belong to the ones who consistently take action in the face of fear, fatigue, and uncertainty. Every powerful transformation you've ever seen in someone's life, business, health, or mindset was initiated and sustained through action.

Without action, nothing moves.

THE POWER OF SMALL, RELENTLESS STEPS

One of the biggest lies we tell ourselves is that big results require big moves, but most of the time, it's not one bold leap that changes your life—it's the compound effect of small, consistent actions.

One honest conversation can repair a broken relationship.

One workout can shift your energy.

One journal entry can create clarity.

One email can change your business trajectory.

We tend to overestimate what we can do in a day and underestimate what we can do in a year of consistent action.

If you want momentum, *act.*

If you want change, *act.*

If you want growth, *act.*

Even when it's uncomfortable.

Especially when it's uncomfortable.

THE PERSONAL STORY — IF I CAN, YOU CAN TOO

I need you to really hear this part.

Because I'm not writing these words from an ivory tower and I'm not some untouchable success story who had it all figured out. I was once lost in every sense of the word.

I spent most of my twenties binge drinking, trapped in cycles of bad habits and broken relationships. I was in emotional shambles. Physically, I was battling Crohn's disease, an invisible monster that wrecked my body and drained my energy. Mentally, I was running on fumes. Spiritually, I was disconnected from purpose.

There was no formal training, no fancy degrees, no roadmap.

I didn't know what leadership development was. I had no background in government. I didn't even know what a podcast was really about when we started ours. I was just a guy trying to put the pieces of his life back together, trying to stop bleeding in areas no one could see, and trying to be someone my daughter could one day look up to.

Then came the moment.

I stopped waiting for confidence, clarity, or the perfect conditions and I started *acting*.

I said yes to opportunities that scared me, I showed up when I didn't feel ready, and I started building something from the inside out.

One uncomfortable rep at a time.

One early morning alarm at a time.

One courageous conversation at a time.

We founded *Action Cultivates Excellence* not because we had it all figured out, but because we didn't—and we knew others didn't either. We committed to the process of becoming better, not just for ourselves, but for our families, our team, and every person we now get to coach, speak to, or write for.

I built this book, these thirty lessons, on the back of action. I'm now privileged to stand on stages and pour into others with power. But don't get it twisted—this all came from the grit of acting when it would've been easier to hide.

If you take nothing else from this chapter—remember this:

If I can, you can too.

No matter how broken, confused, or behind you feel—action is the doorway to a new life.

REAL-WORLD LEGACY: THE POWER OF TAKING ACTION

Let's zoom out for a moment.

Howard Schultz, the former CEO of Starbucks, grew up in public housing in Brooklyn with no silver spoon and no trust fund. What he had though, was a relentless work ethic and the courage to take action. After a trip to Italy, he was inspired by the café culture and envisioned something bigger than just selling coffee—he saw a third place between work and home.

People doubted him and investors laughed, but he acted.

He didn't just pitch the idea, he poured himself into it, took out loans, bought the company, and began building one store at a time. Starbucks didn't become a global brand overnight. It became what it is today because Schultz kept acting on his vision, even when others couldn't see it.

Action is what transforms vision into legacy.

HOW TO MAKE ACTION A DAILY HABIT

You don't need to change your entire life today, you just need to start.

Here's how:

- Shrink the gap between decision and execution. Don't give yourself time to overthink. Choose, then act.
- Set a 3-action rule. No matter how busy the day gets, do three meaningful things aligned with your goals, every single day.
- Celebrate the doing and stop obsessing over outcomes. Winning is in the showing up and executing—period.

HOW ACTION TRANSFORMS YOUR LEADERSHIP

It builds trust. People follow leaders who take initiative and follow through—not just talk.

It creates confidence. Action breeds clarity. Every time you take a step forward, even if it's messy, you reinforce belief in yourself.

It sets the tone. Your team, your kids, your peers—they don't listen to what you say, they mirror what you *do*.

It fuels growth. Every challenge you lean into becomes fuel for your next level.

FINAL THOUGHT

This entire book, this entire journey—it only means something if you use it.

The only thing separating you from the life you want is consistent action.

Not talent, not luck, and not time. *Action*.

This isn't the end—it's the ignition point.

You now hold the lessons.

You have the truth.

You've felt the power of becoming better.

Now go live it.

ACTION STEP

You've made it through all thirty lessons.

Now ask yourself, *"What's the thing I've been avoiding?"*

"The conversation I haven't had?"

"The change I haven't started?"

"The vision I haven't pursued?"

Today, take one bold, unapologetic action toward it.

It doesn't matter how small—just make sure it's forward.

REFLECTION QUESTION

When I look in the mirror a year from now, what steps will I have needed to take in order to respect the person staring back at me?

AFTERWORD

Leadership isn't a title you earn once.

It's a decision you make—**every damn day**.

To show up, to grow up, and to lead forward, even when no one's watching, and *especially* when no one's clapping.

You've just finished thirty lessons. It's not the end of the road, it's a checkpoint, a mirror, and a spark.

Leadership isn't something you master once and for all, it's something you practice over and over. In the quiet, in the chaos, and in the moments when it would be easier to coast, you continue moving forward.

Let's be honest, we all feel that pull.

To relax once we've made it somewhere, to stop pushing when things are "good enough," and to believe that growth is for the beginners, "We're beyond that now," we tell ourselves.

But here's the truth most people *won't* tell you:

The moment you stop leading yourself is the moment you start declining.

Not all at once and not in one dramatic crash.

It'll happen in small, quiet ways:

• You skip that hard conversation

• You ignore the misalignment

• You stop reflecting

• You trade challenge for comfort

• You settle

Then one day, you wake up and wonder how the hell you got so far from the fire that once lit you up.

Not you though.

Not anymore.

You didn't read this book just for inspiration. You read it to raise your standard—for your team, your family, your body, your mindset, your mission.

You're in this for life.

That means when the lessons feel hard, you revisit them.

When the world gets loud, you come back to your clarity.

When you drift, you realign.

When you fall short, you recalibrate. **You don't quit.**

The best leaders don't aim for perfection, they aim for consistency with direction.

So, take what you've learned—and live it.

Bleed it into your calendar, your communication, your discipline, and your presence.

People are watching—your kids, your coworkers, your partner, and your community.

More than that—*you're* watching.

At the end of the day, leadership is about being someone you respect in the mirror and someone you can count on when it matters.

Here's your final lesson—the one that isn't numbered:

Leadership is forever.

Keep showing up, keep reflecting, and keep leading.

Because the second you stop is the second it all starts slipping.

You didn't come this far just to coast.

Let's lead—for real and for good.

Let's build something that outlasts us.

ACKNOWLEDGMENTS

This book isn't mine alone. It's the product of every win and loss, every lesson learned, and every person who stood beside me through it all.

First and always—Thank You, God.

Without You, none of this would exist. You gave me a voice shaped by trials, a platform to use it for something bigger than myself, and a purpose rooted in love and service. I'm far from perfect, but I am committed to walking the path You've laid out—leading with humility, serving with grace, and living as Your disciple. Thank You for never giving up on me, even when I tried to give up on myself. I pray this book reaches hearts, inspiring people not just to lead, but to lead with meaning and purpose. All glory to You.

To my daughter, Kali —

You are the heartbeat behind every word. Your laughter, your energy, your curiosity—they remind me every day why I fight to be better. You've taught me more about real leadership than any book or coach ever could. Strength in gentleness and power in presence. The true measure of a man is how he treats those he loves when no one else is watching. I lead so I can be the dad you deserve. My deepest hope is that you grow up seeing love, discipline, faith, and integrity lived out in our home. I love you beyond words.

To my parents, Nanci and Michael —

You gave me everything I needed, even when the path wasn't easy. Mom, your resilience through the darkest seasons showed me what real strength looks like—choosing growth when giving up would have been easier. Dad, your relentless work ethic and sacrifice shaped not only my grind but also my heart. I am proud to be your oldest son, and I hope I make you both proud every day.

To my siblings, Danielle and Matthew —

We weathered the same storms, and that bond runs deep. Danielle, the way you pour into your students is leadership in its purest form—selfless, consistent, and full of love. Matthew, your drive and discipline remind me what quiet strength looks like. You've built your path with integrity and focus, and I'm proud of the man you've become. The three of us didn't just survive — we grew stronger together. Team Reggina, always.

To Katherine Cepeda —

Thank you for coming back into my life right when I needed you most. Your faith, your strength, and your love have challenged me to be a better man, leader, and partner. You hold me accountable with love and believe in me when I forget how to believe in myself. I'm so excited for our future—our faith, our love, and the life we're building together. I love you deeply.

To My Grandparents —

Though you've all gone home to heaven, your love, lessons, and legacy live on in me. I carry your strength, your faith, and your values into everything I do. I hope I'm making you proud.

To Doreen Roman —

Your support never wavered. I made more mistakes than I can count, but you never turned your back on me. You stood by my side with patience, loyalty, and love. Thank you for believing in me through it all.

To Commissioner Kathleen O'Connor —

Thank you for seeing something in me when I was just twenty years old and barely believing in myself. You challenged me to step up and speak, and that moment changed everything. Your leadership and mentorship set a standard I carry with me every day. I will never forget the seed you planted.

To Kevin Cook —

Thank you for empowering me throughout my journey in public service. For over twenty years, you've invested in me and believed in my potential. Your mentorship has been a cornerstone of my growth as both a leader and a person.

To Commissioner Andre Early —

Thank you for taking a chance on me when I thought I had it all figured out. You called me a leader before I even earned the title, and that belief changed everything. You taught me that leadership is about planting roots, showing up, and creating opportunities for others. Your trust shaped how I lead today.

To Commissioner Terrance Jackson —

Serving as your Deputy Commissioner has been one of the greatest honors of my life. You empowered me, trusted me, and developed me without micromanaging. You led not just with authority but with heart. Because of you, I became the man and leader I was meant to be. Thank you for your trust, your lessons, and your friendship.

To my Godchildren, Mason and Hailee —

You hold a special place in my heart. Watching you grow reminds me of the responsibility and privilege leadership carries across generations. I hope to be a steady guide and presence as you find your own voice and path. Always know you are deeply loved and believed in.

To my Greenburgh Team —

Serving Greenburgh is an honor. The legacy of the leaders before me laid the foundation, and together we pushed it forward. The first decade shaped me as a leader and as a man—I found clarity, purpose, and family. Thank you for believing in the vision and allowing me to serve our community.

To Mark Carter, Ozzy Bobe, and Angelo LaRoche —

Brothers for life. We've been through everything—the highs, the heartbreaks, the breakthroughs, and the breakdowns. Life tried to break us, but we kept showing up for each other. That loyalty, those late-night talks, those shared scars—it all built a bond I will carry forever. I love you men, always.

To Claudio Valenzuela and the entire No Snooze community —

No Snooze wasn't just a podcast—it became a movement. Claudio, thank you for being my brother in the grind, my anchor, my shooter, and my partner. We turned real conversations into a lasting legacy. Mike Parelli—thank you for starting this journey with me and co-hosting for the first three years. To the entire No Snooze family— thank you for believing, for showing up, and for living the message. You've proven that ordinary people can do extraordinary things by simply refusing to hit snooze. **Snooze on life?** *Never that.*

To Sean Degnan and the Action Cultivates Excellence (A.C.E.) community —

Thank you. We're changing the world by showing strength and vulnerability can coexist. Sean, you are the best leader I know—your vision and belief in the mission pushed me to rise again. To the

A.C.E. community, thank you for proving real leaders lead with both strength and heart. We're building something that will outlast us.

To Erwin Gilliam —

More than just my barber, you were the first man to see the man of God in me before I even saw it myself. Your quiet faith, steady presence, and genuine care helped shape my spiritual journey in ways words can hardly capture. Thank you for believing in me, grounding me, and reminding me of who I truly am.

To Mary Bellettieri —

Thank you for your wisdom, guidance, and heart throughout this process. Your belief in this message never wavered, and I am beyond grateful. I couldn't have done this without you. Here's to many more moments of impact together.

To You, The Reader —

Thank you for choosing to walk this path with me. Leadership isn't given—it's built lesson by lesson, step by step, sometimes painfully. By picking up this book, you've chosen to show up, to grow, and to lead. I see you. I respect your courage. May these lessons inspire you to lead from the inside out. Here's to your breakthrough.

ABOUT THE AUTHOR

Dave Reggina is a leadership expert, keynote speaker, and Deputy Commissioner in the largest town in Westchester County, NY. He's also the co-founder of A.C.E. (Action Cultivates Excellence)—an exclusive, transformative experience for those committed to achieving personal and professional growth. As host of The *No Snooze Podcast*, a top-ranked show globally on Spotify, Dave speaks directly to high performers seeking more clarity, ownership, and momentum in their lives.

Dave's story is far from conventional. He was raised in a culturally blended home—his mother Jewish, his father Italian—in a world full of contradictions, love and instability, adversity and resilience. By age thirteen, he was already juggling two jobs, loading propane tanks into cars and caddying on golf courses, learning early that leadership means showing up, regardless of your circumstances.

As a teenager, Dave was diagnosed with Crohn's disease, dropping forty pounds in four months. He walked the halls of high school with toilet paper in his backpack and a pain most couldn't see. Doctors told him he'd live with the illness for life but that diagnosis ignited his first true leadership journey. Dave became obsessed with health and wellness—reading books, tracking symptoms, building nutrition plans, and designing his own fitness routines. He was reshaping his life even while silently battling body dysmorphia, something he continues to work through today.

Though life at home was rooted in love, it was also unpredictable. Dave moved ten times before graduating high school, constantly learning how to adapt and keep moving forward. It was a near-tragic moment with his mother—a moment where he almost lost her—that cracked him wide open. That rock-bottom season became the root of his transformation and the foundation for his belief, leadership starts by leading yourself through life's hardest moments.

In early 2025, Dave was listed as high risk for colon cancer after a routine colonoscopy. It was another test—but this time, he approached it with the same conviction that had shaped his life. By the grace of God, the results came back negative. To Dave, it only confirmed what he already knew, that most people don't break down because of what they're faced with—they break down because of *what they do* with what they're faced with.

Over the past decade, Dave's leadership journey has accelerated. At age 26, he became New York State's youngest appointed Commissioner. He was named a Top 30 Under 30 recipient in 2019 and has been featured in major publications including Yahoo, U.S. Business News, and the Star Tribune. In 2024, he served as a judge for seven hundred entrepreneurs at Invest Fest in Atlanta, Georgia, helping award the $100,000 Nipsey Hussle Business Grant sponsored by Microsoft, Earn Your Leisure, and The Neighborhood Nip Foundation. The following year in 2025, he returned as a keynote speaker alongside billionaires, Magic Johnson and Jack Dorsey.

Dave leads teams of twenty five to three hundred in government and is the proud father of his daughter, Kali. His mission is clear—to build leaders who first lead themselves, then lead others. 30 Lessons to

Lead isn't a highlight reel—it's a roadmap forged through fire and it will challenge you to lead your own life, from wherever you are, *right now*.

Connect with Dave at www.davereggina.com

Follow Dave Reggina: @daveregg
Follow the No Snooze Podcast: @nosnoozepodcast
Follow Action Cultivates Excellence: @acesanctuary